THE WONDERFUL DOGS COLORING BOOK

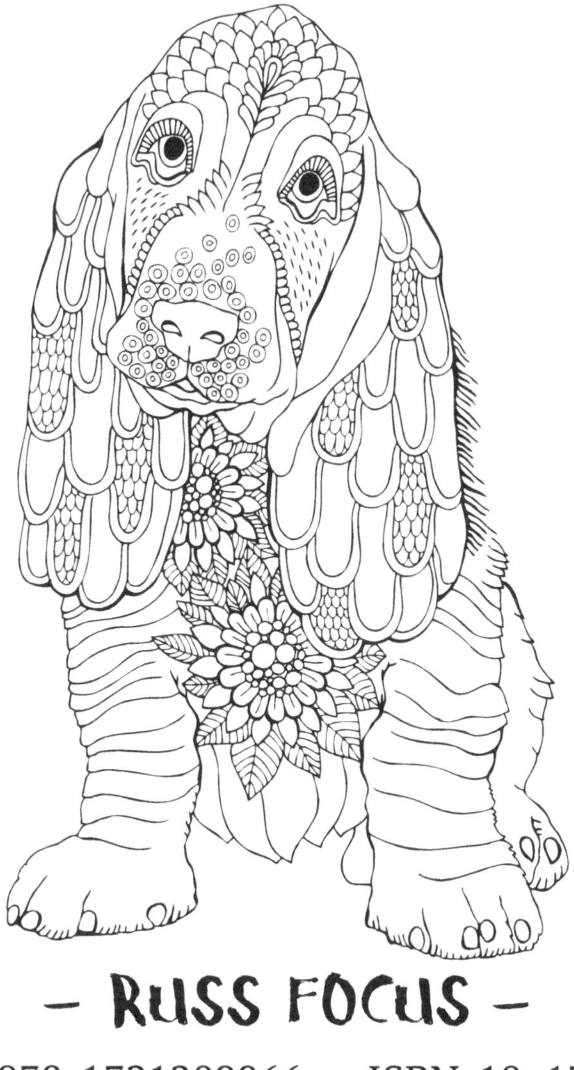

- RUSS FOCUS -

ISBN-13: 978-1721209866 ISBN-10: 1721209867
PUBLISHED BY RUSS FOCUS PUBLISHED IN USA

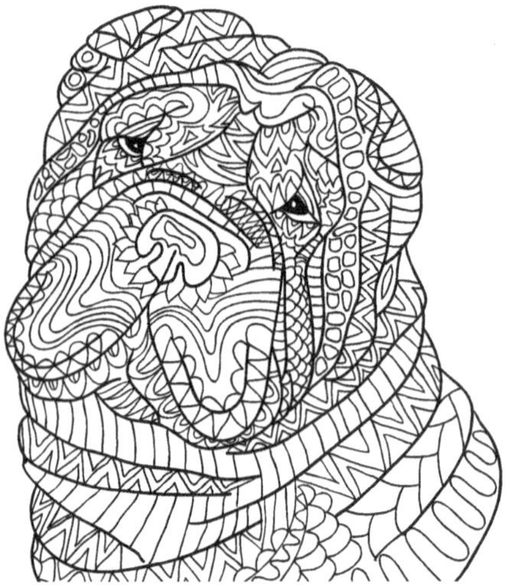

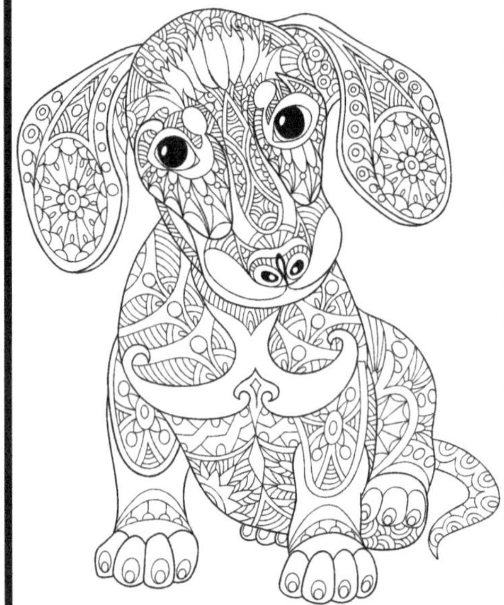

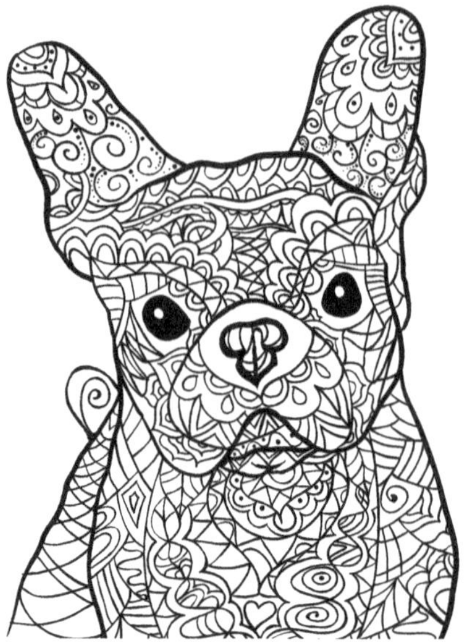

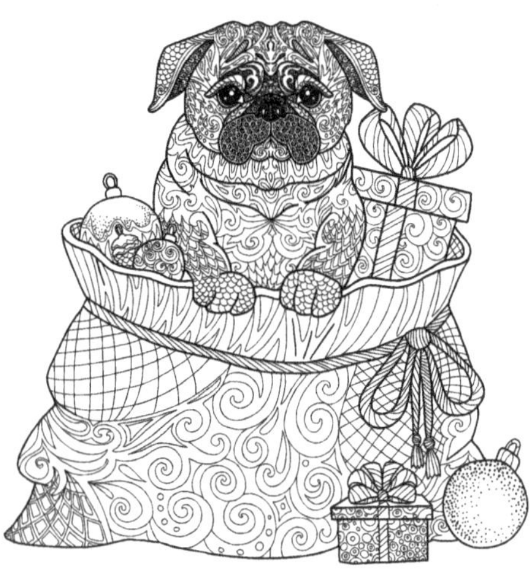

SAMPLE
DOG
COLORING
17 of 42
PAGES

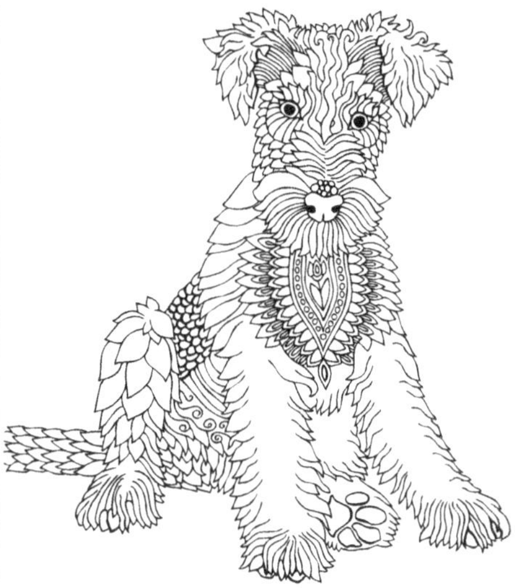

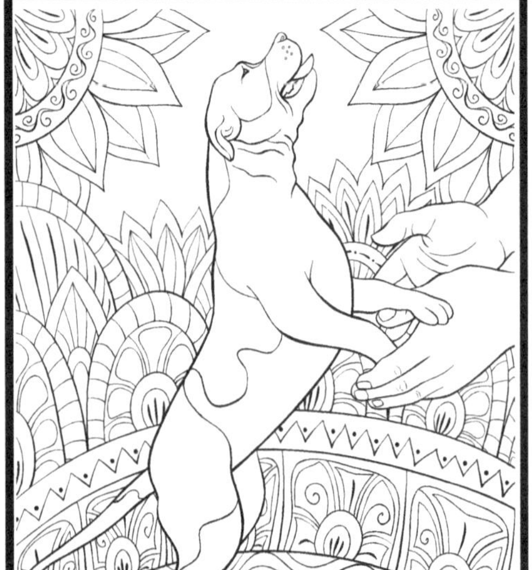

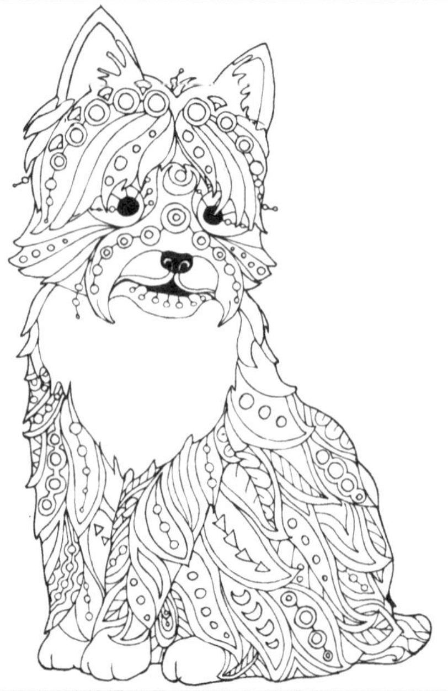

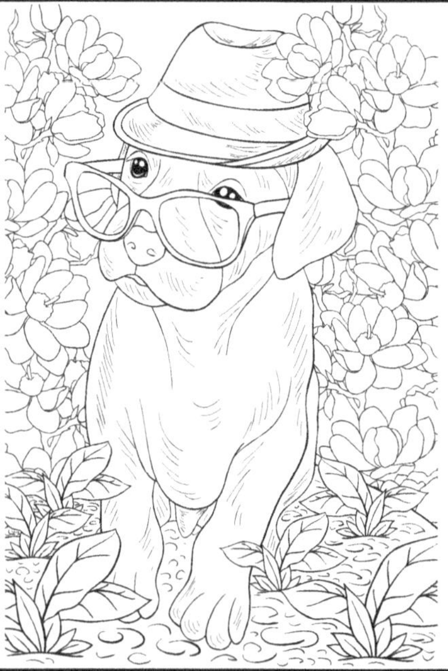

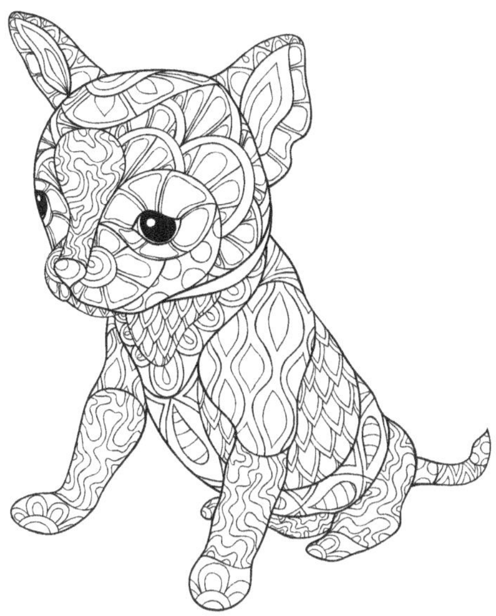
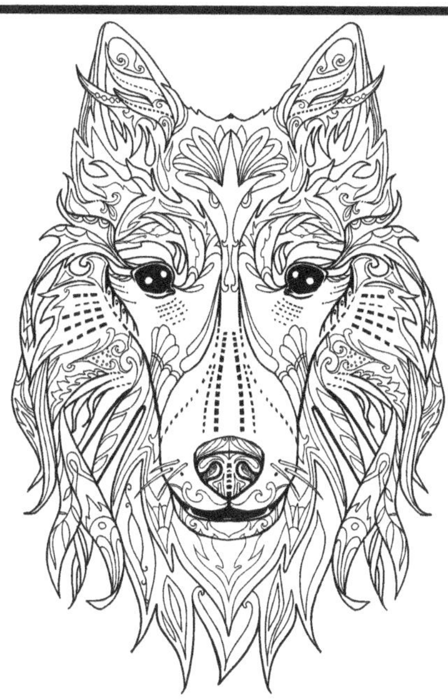
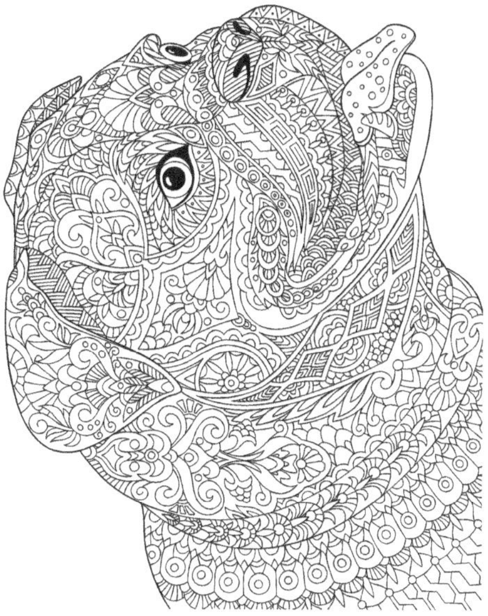
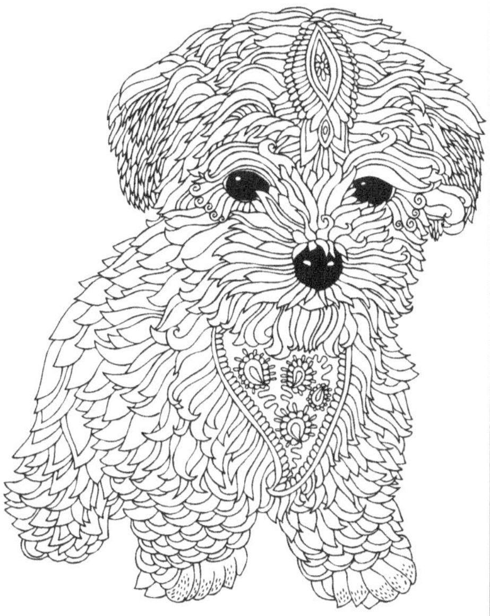
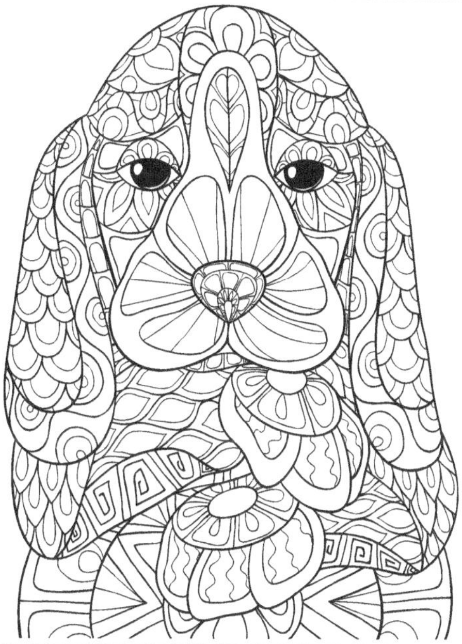
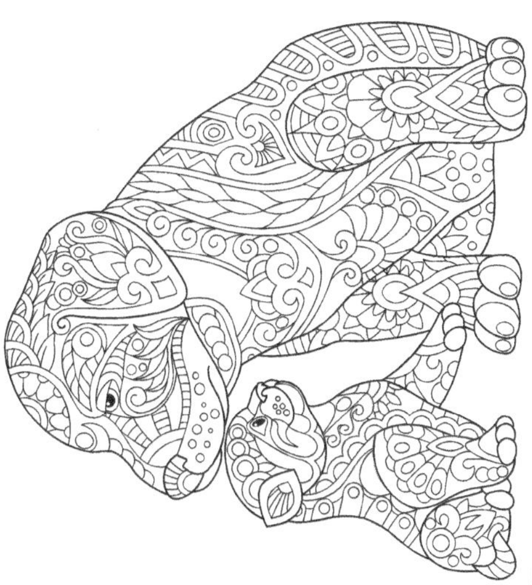
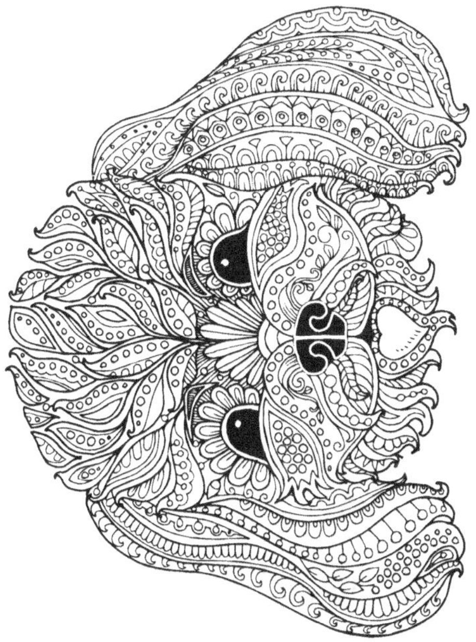
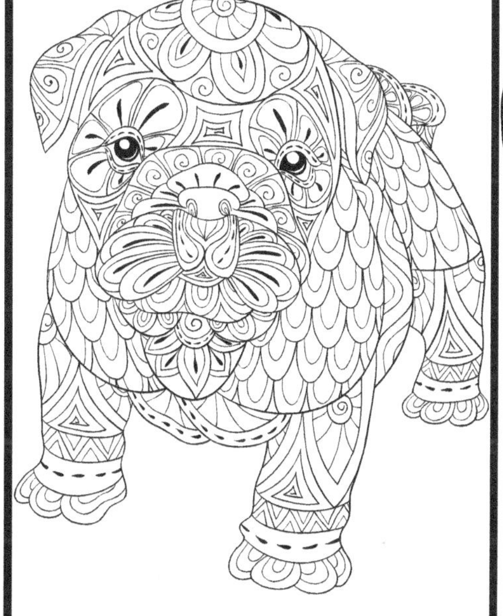
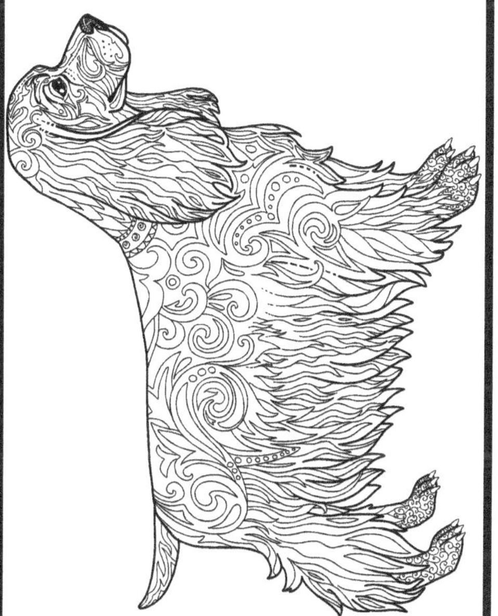

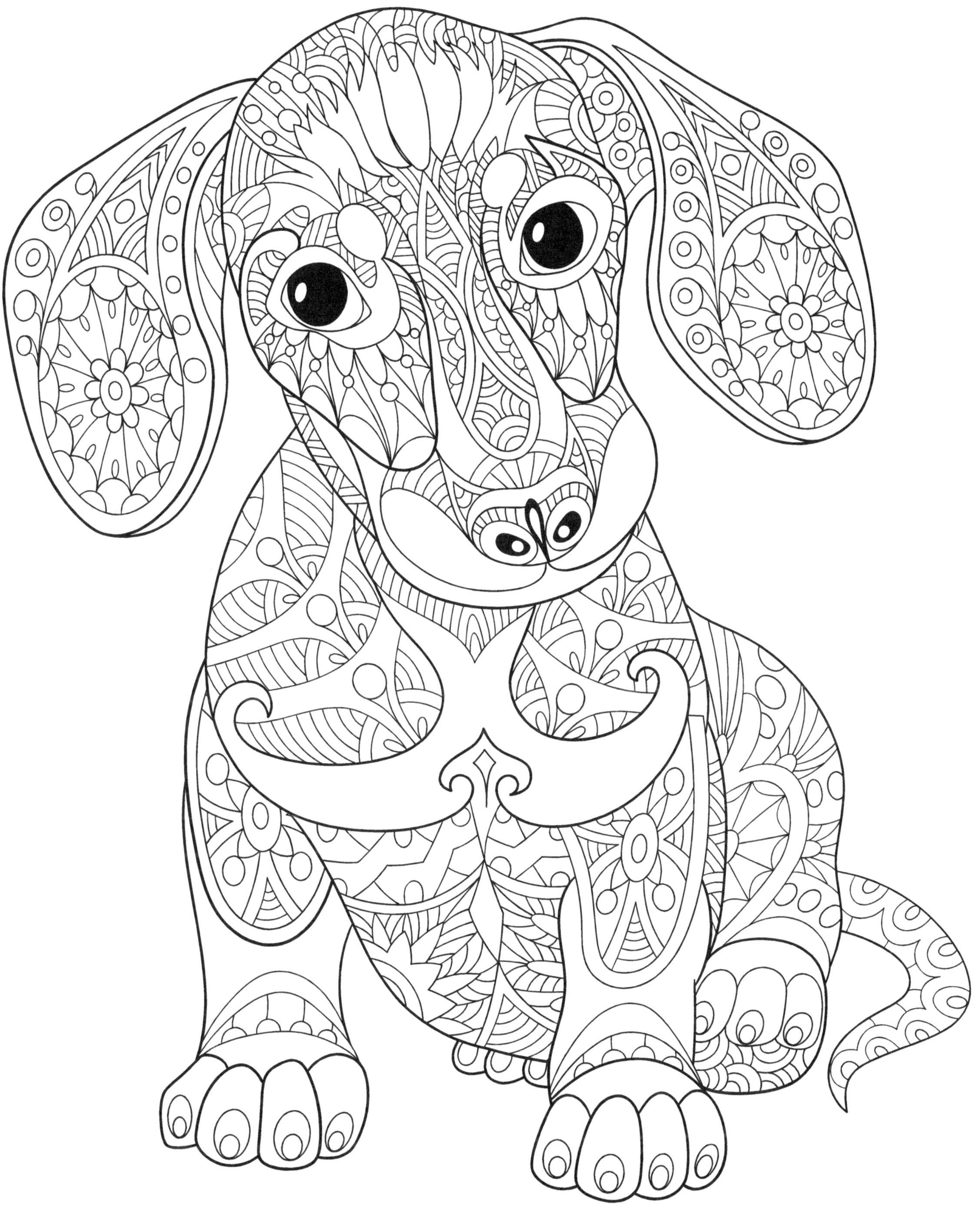

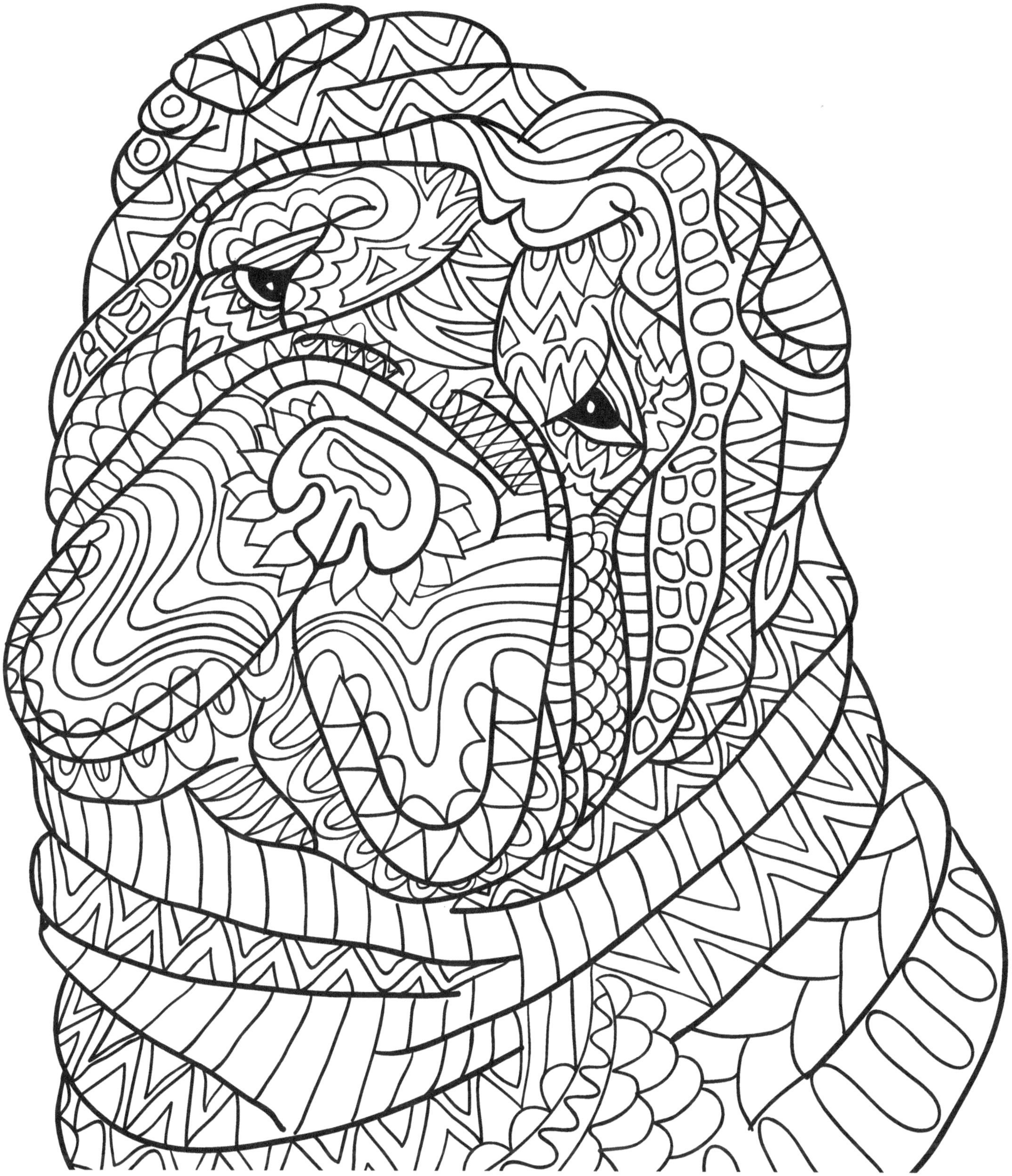

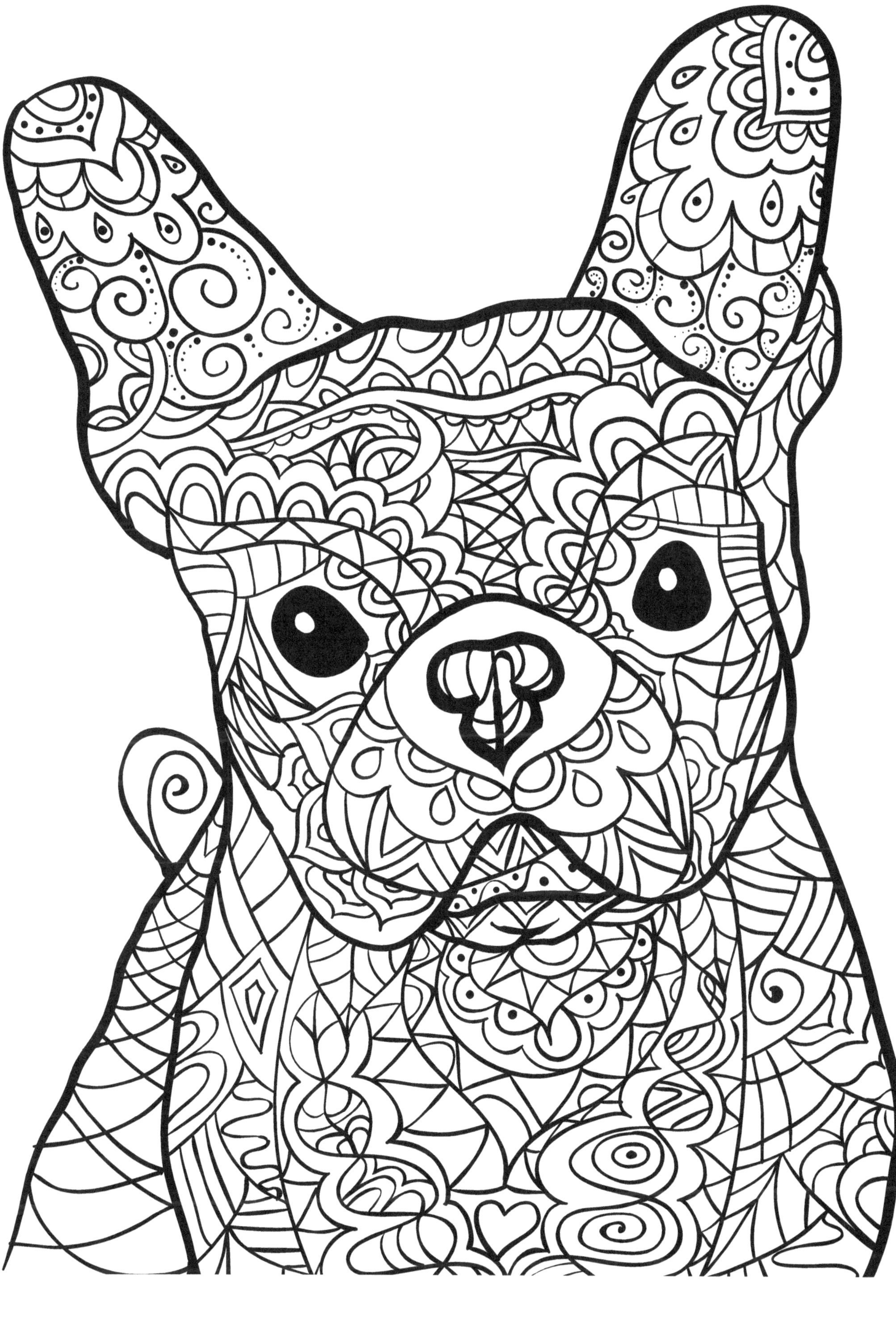

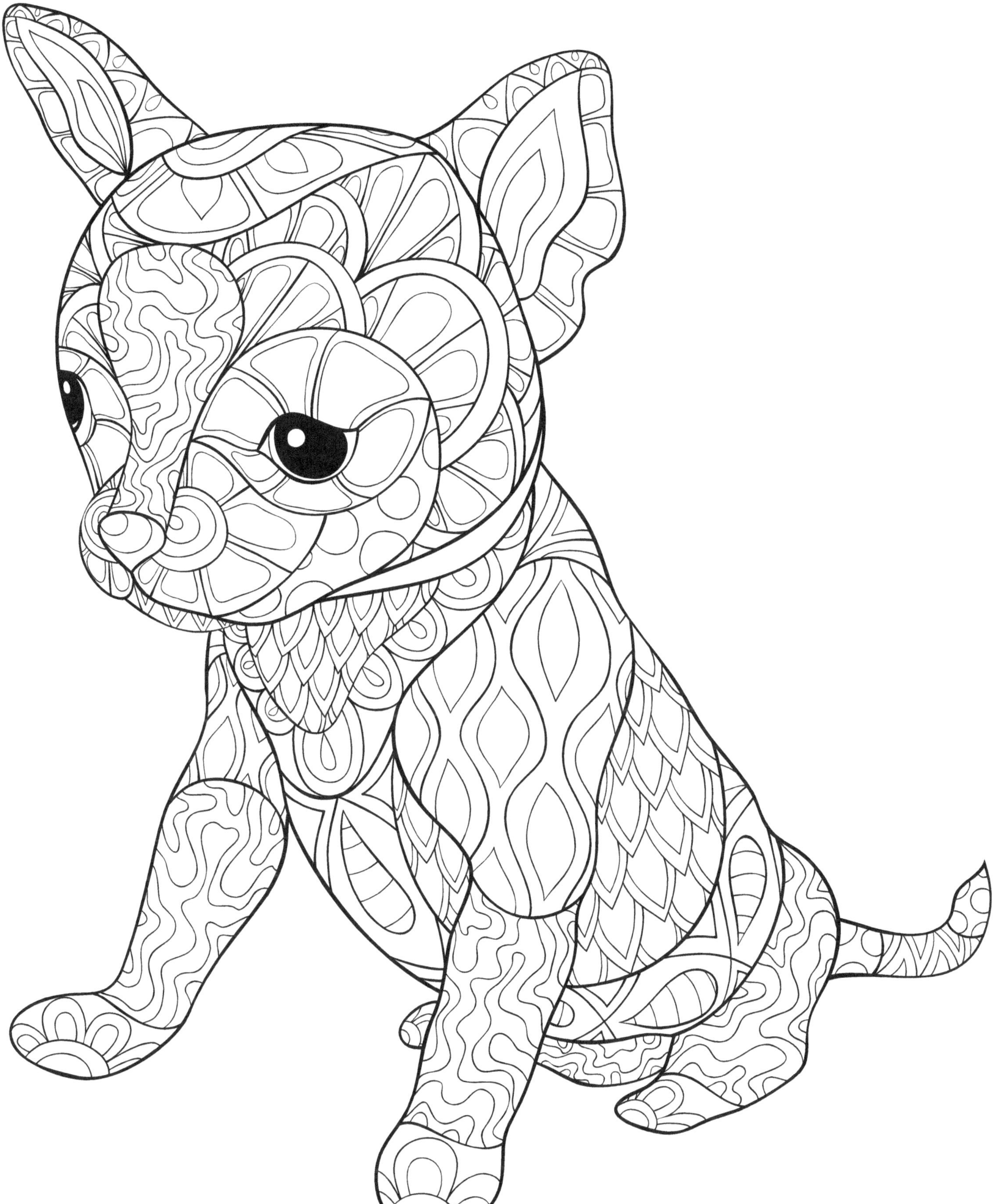

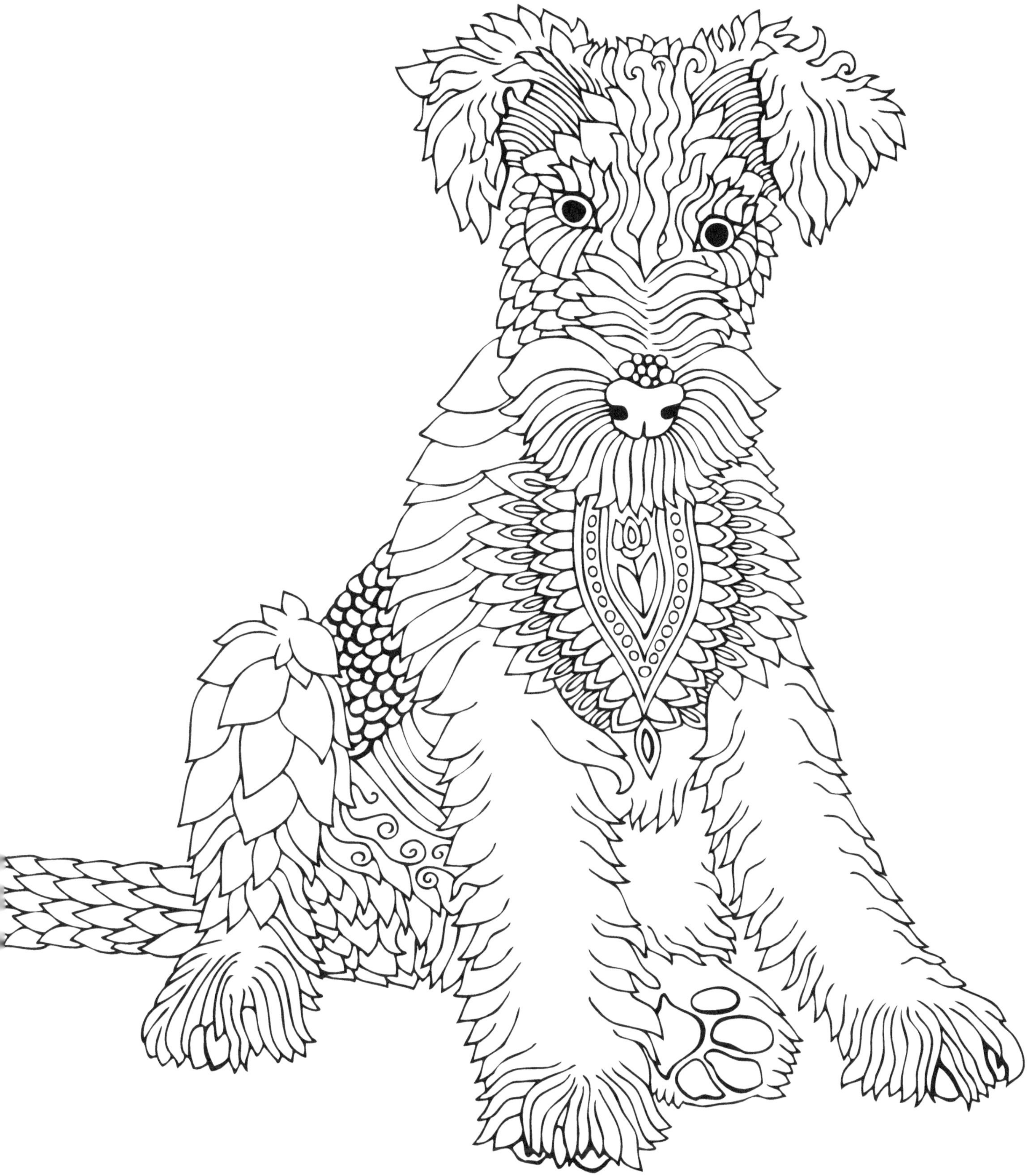

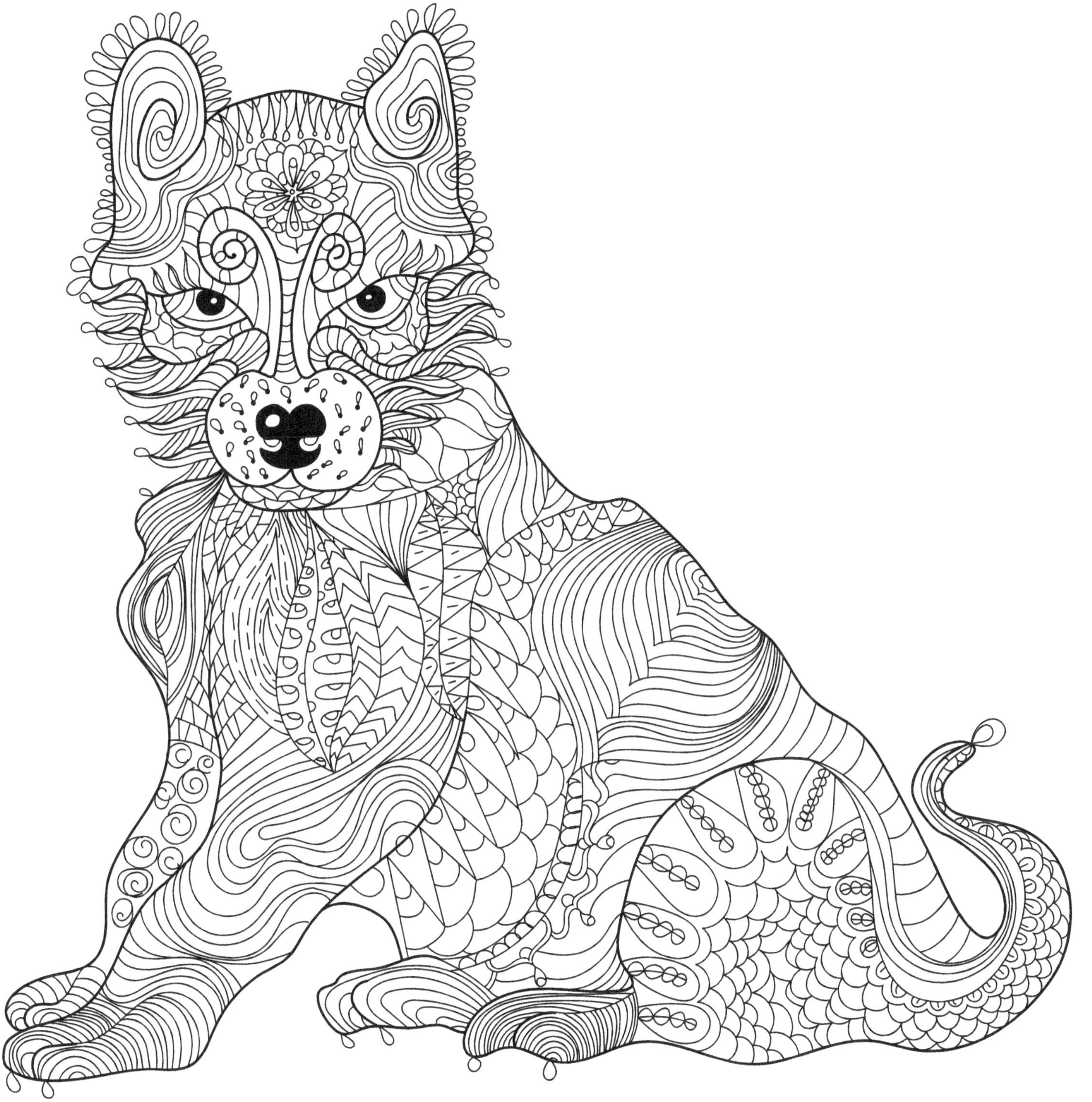

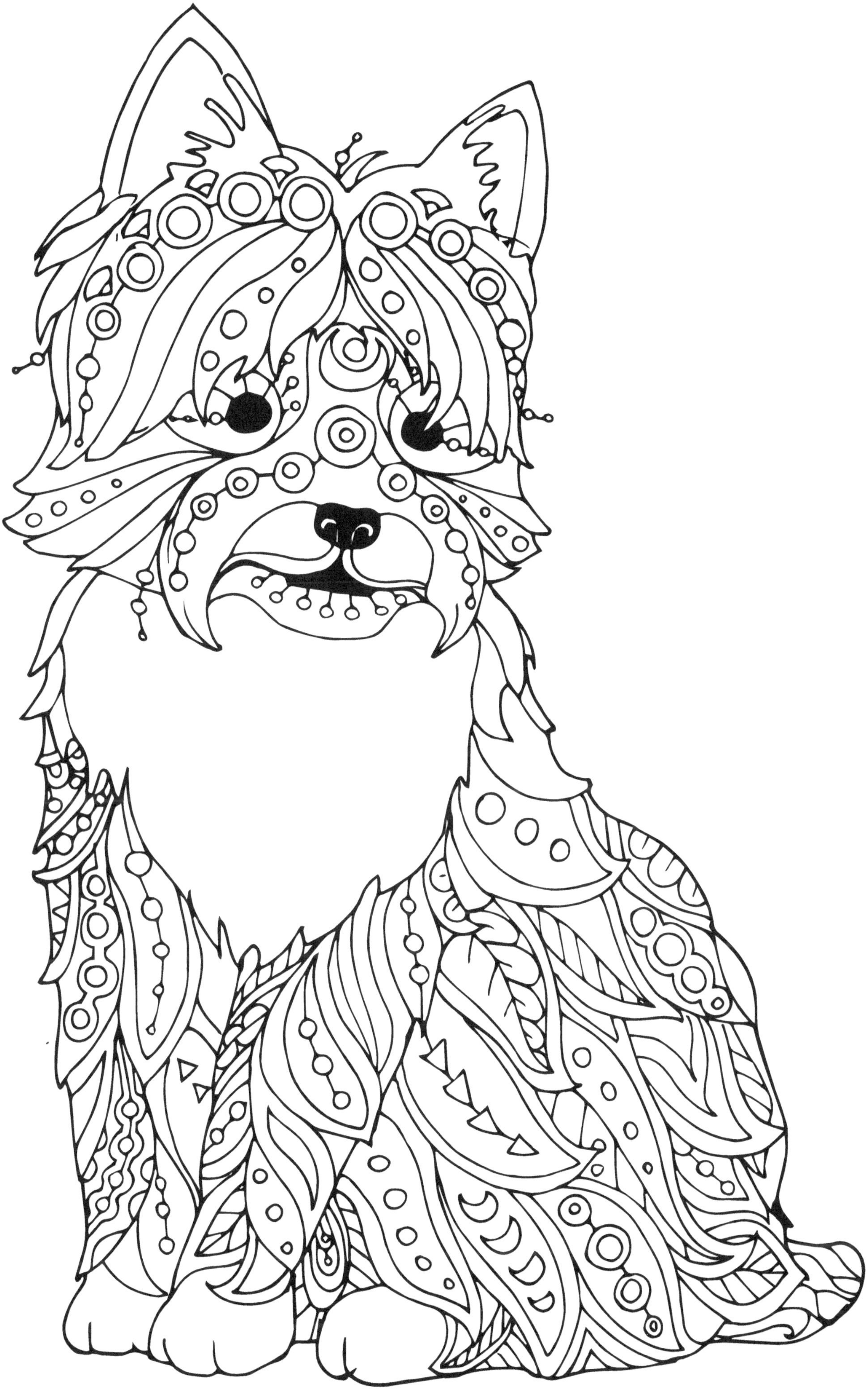

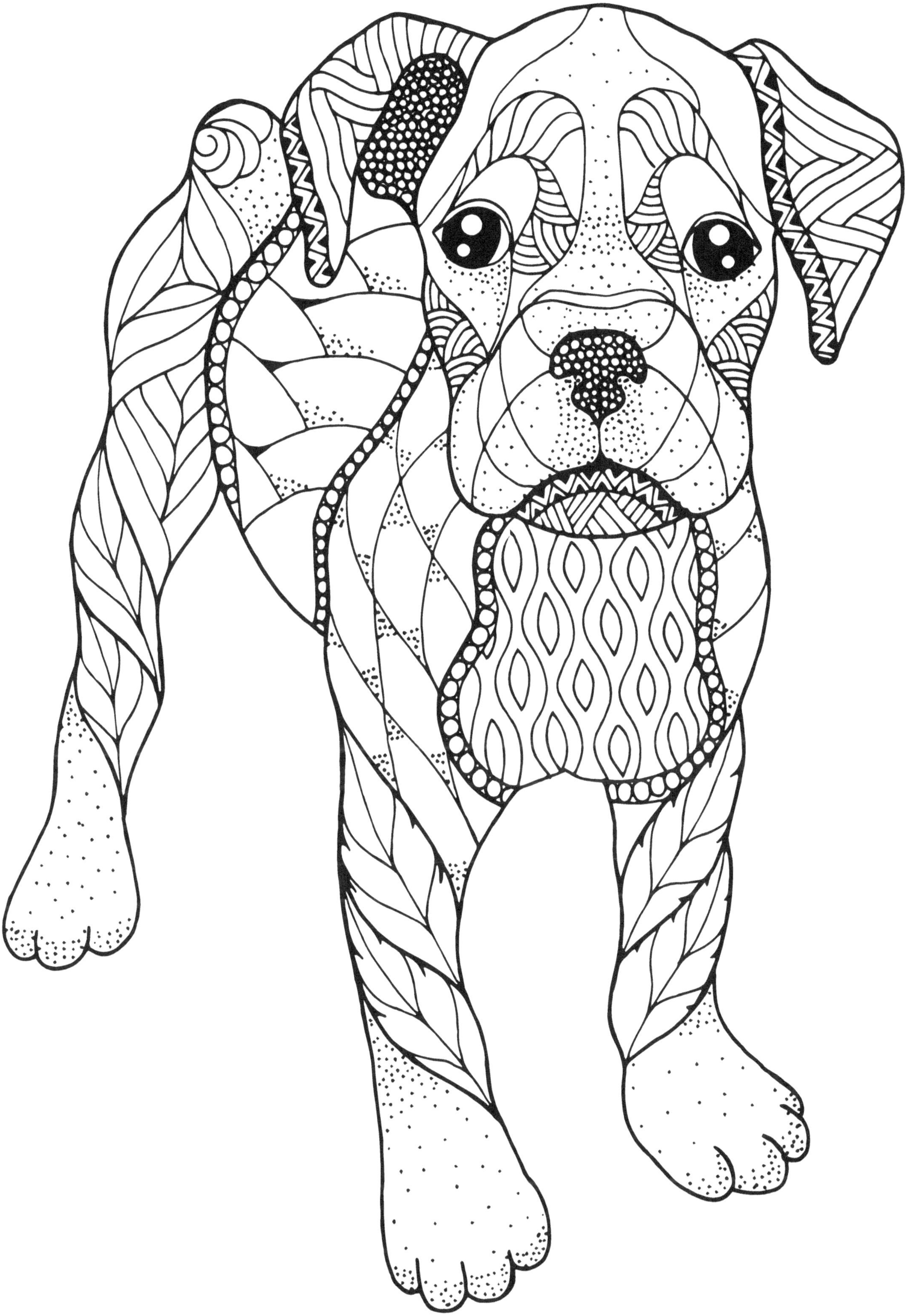

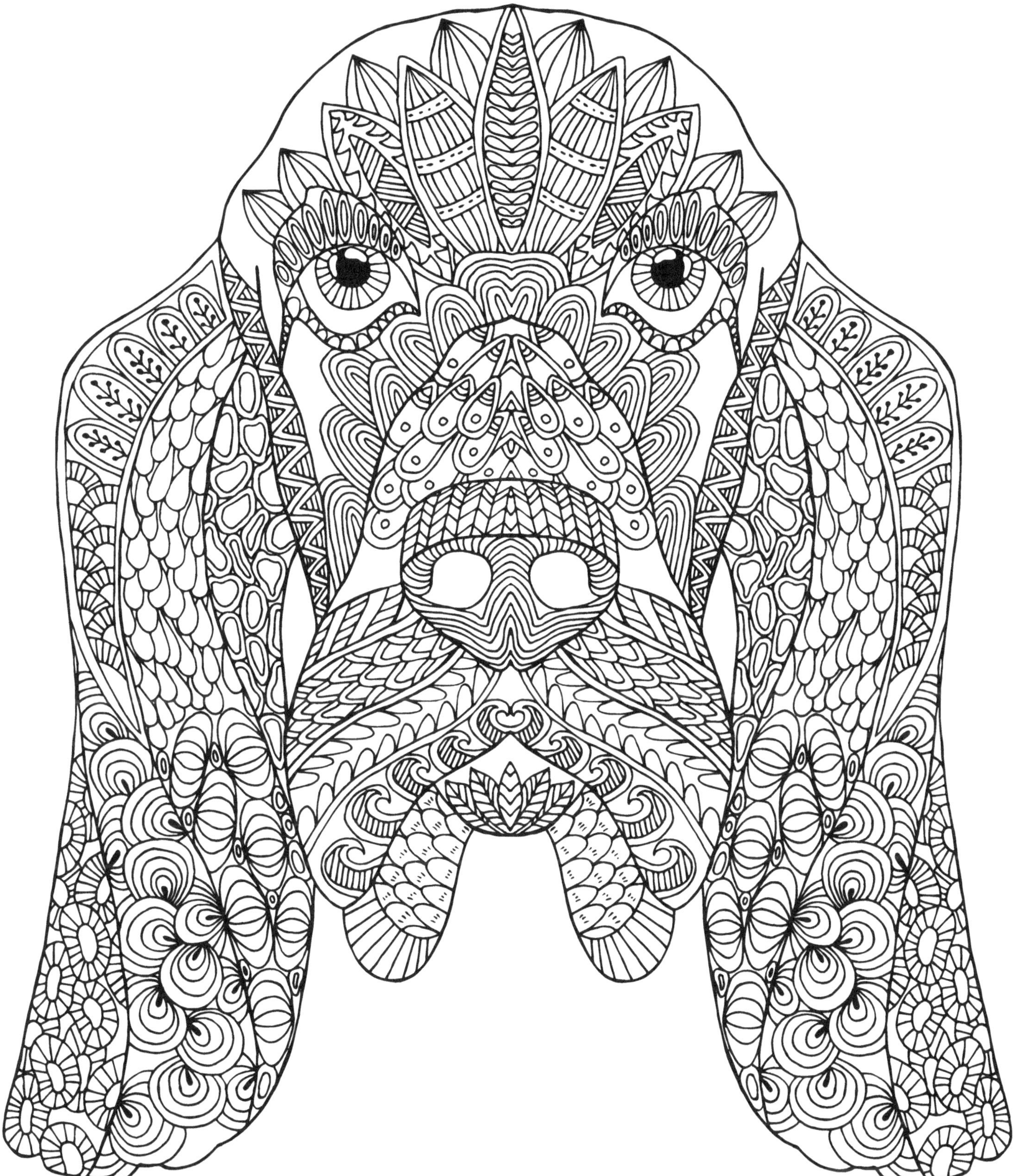

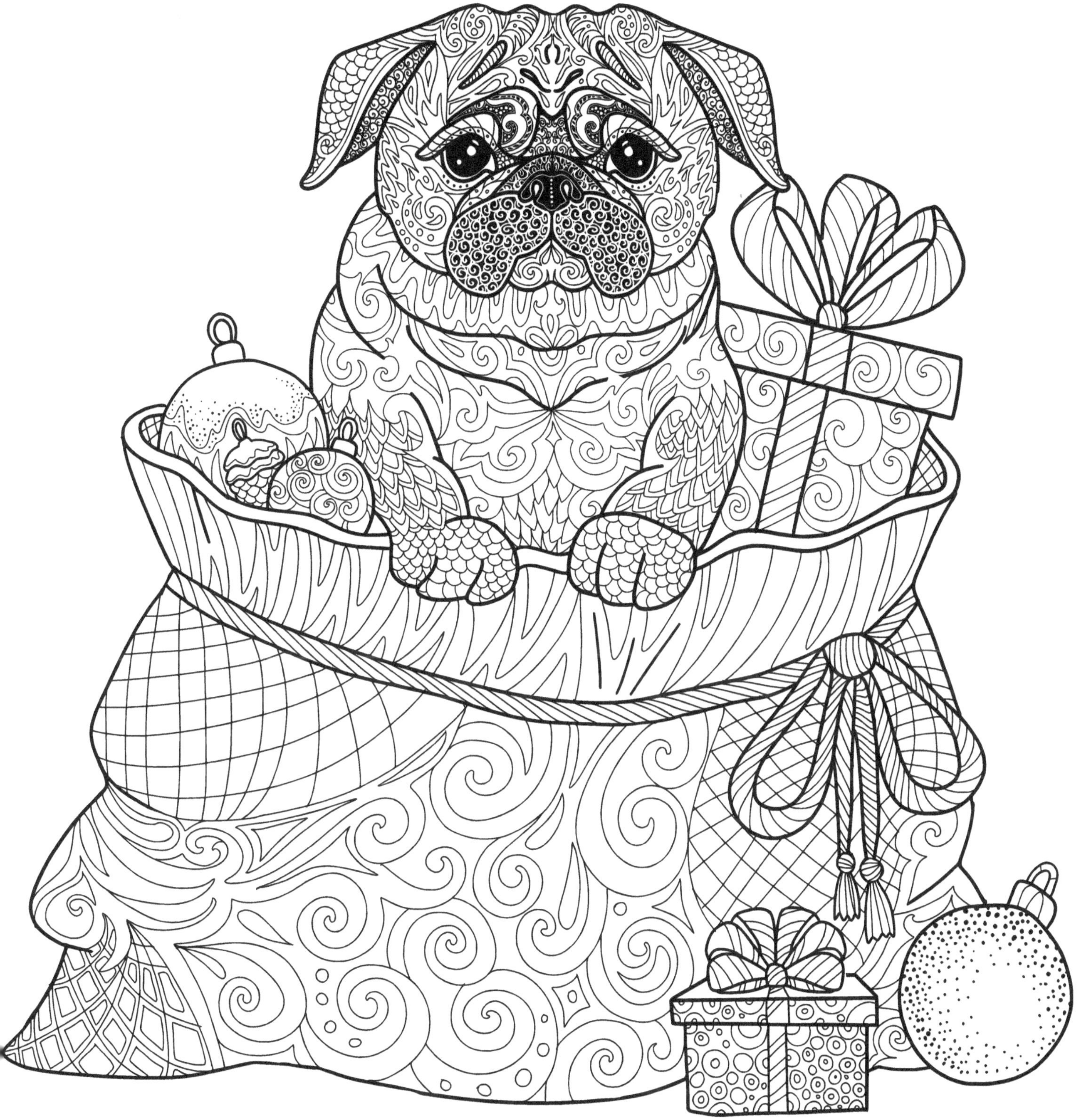

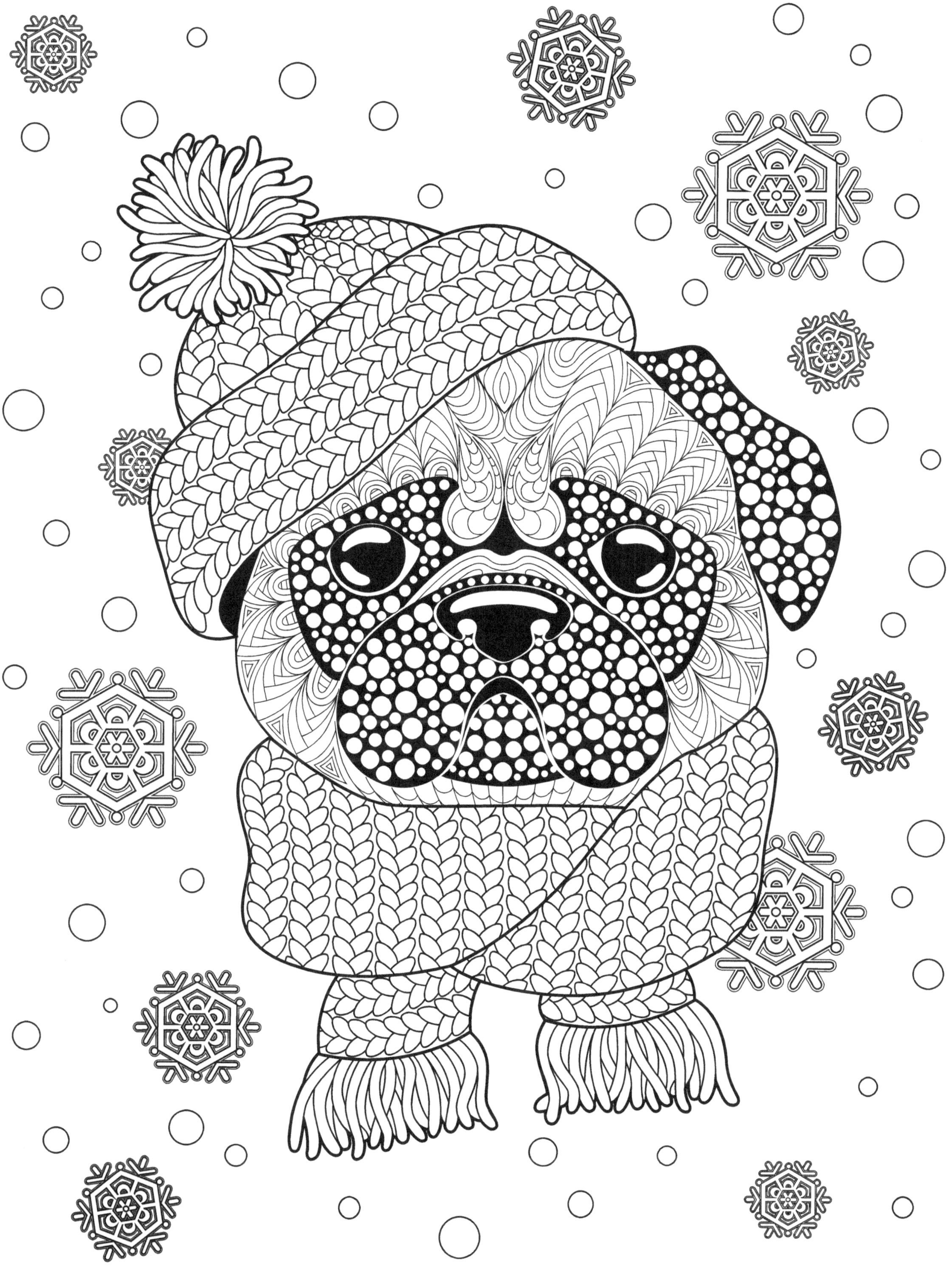

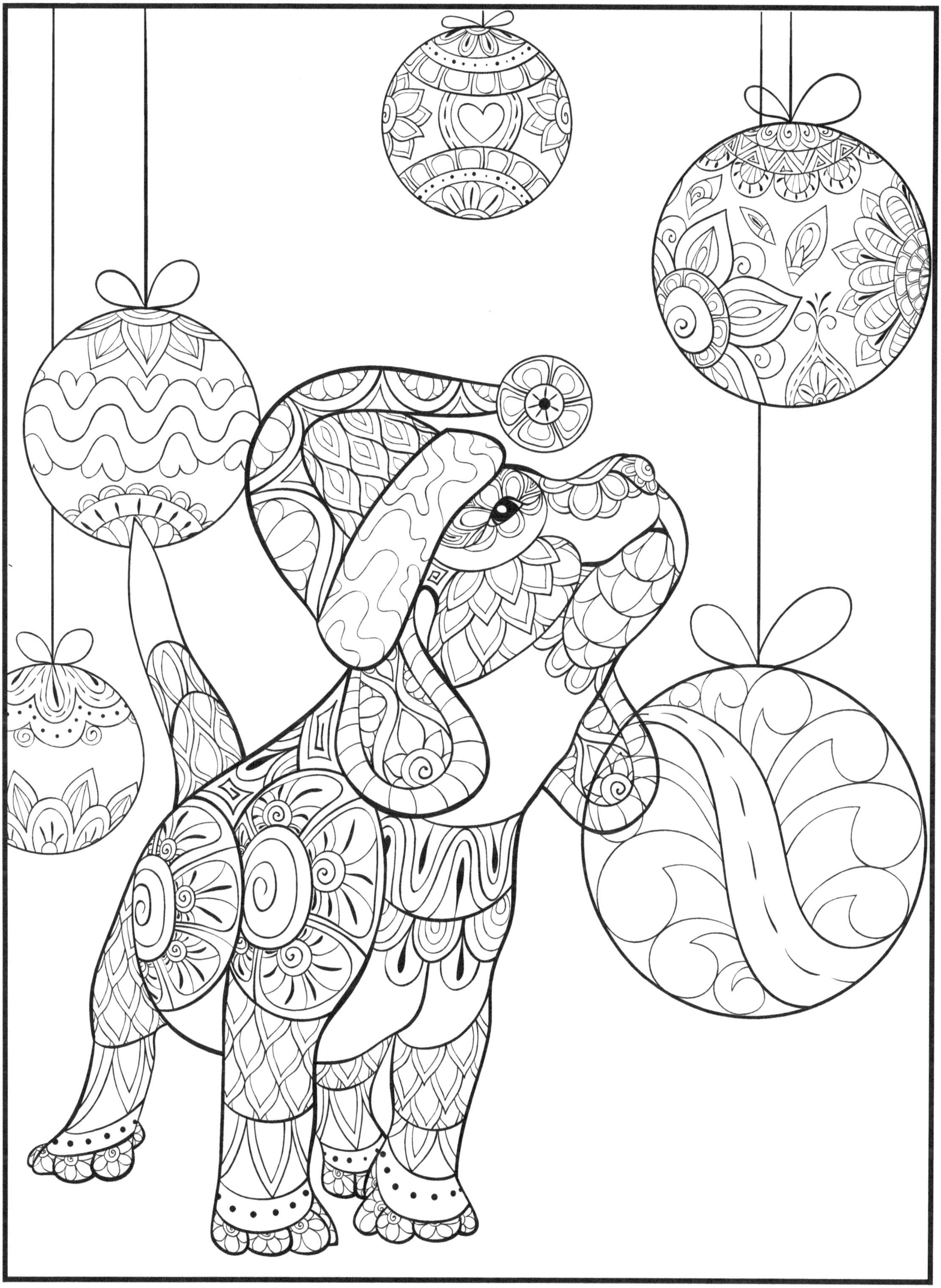

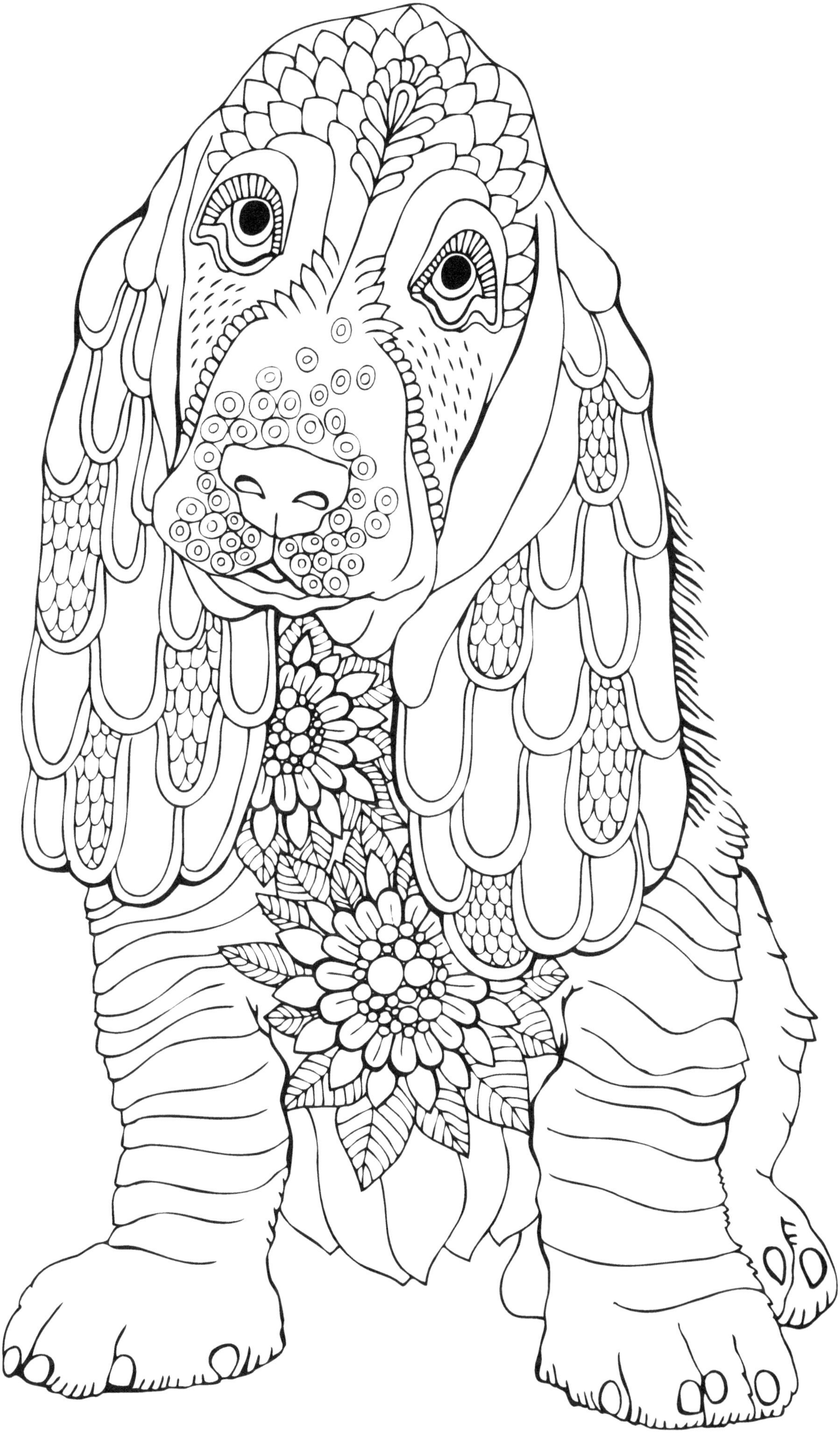

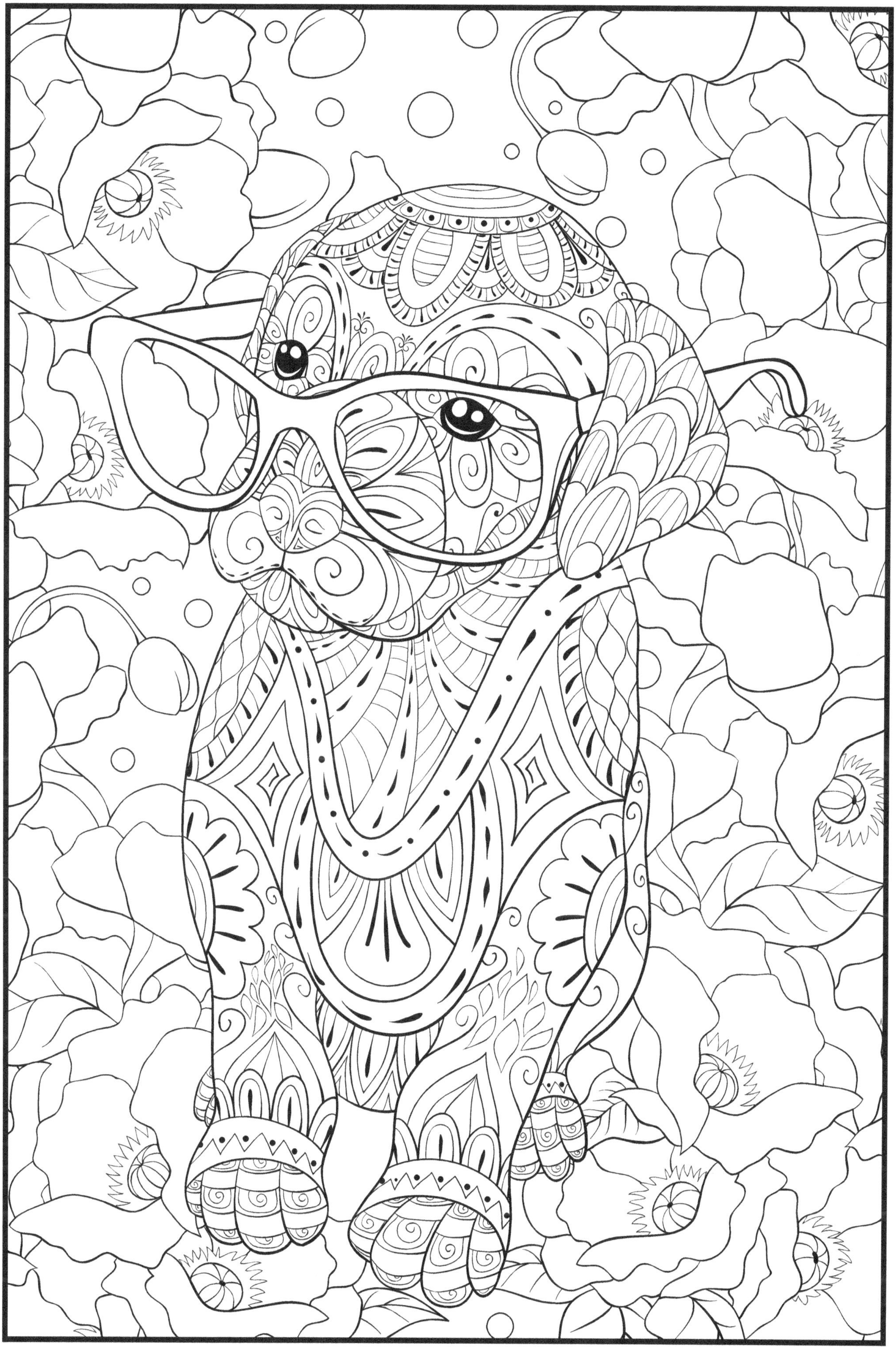

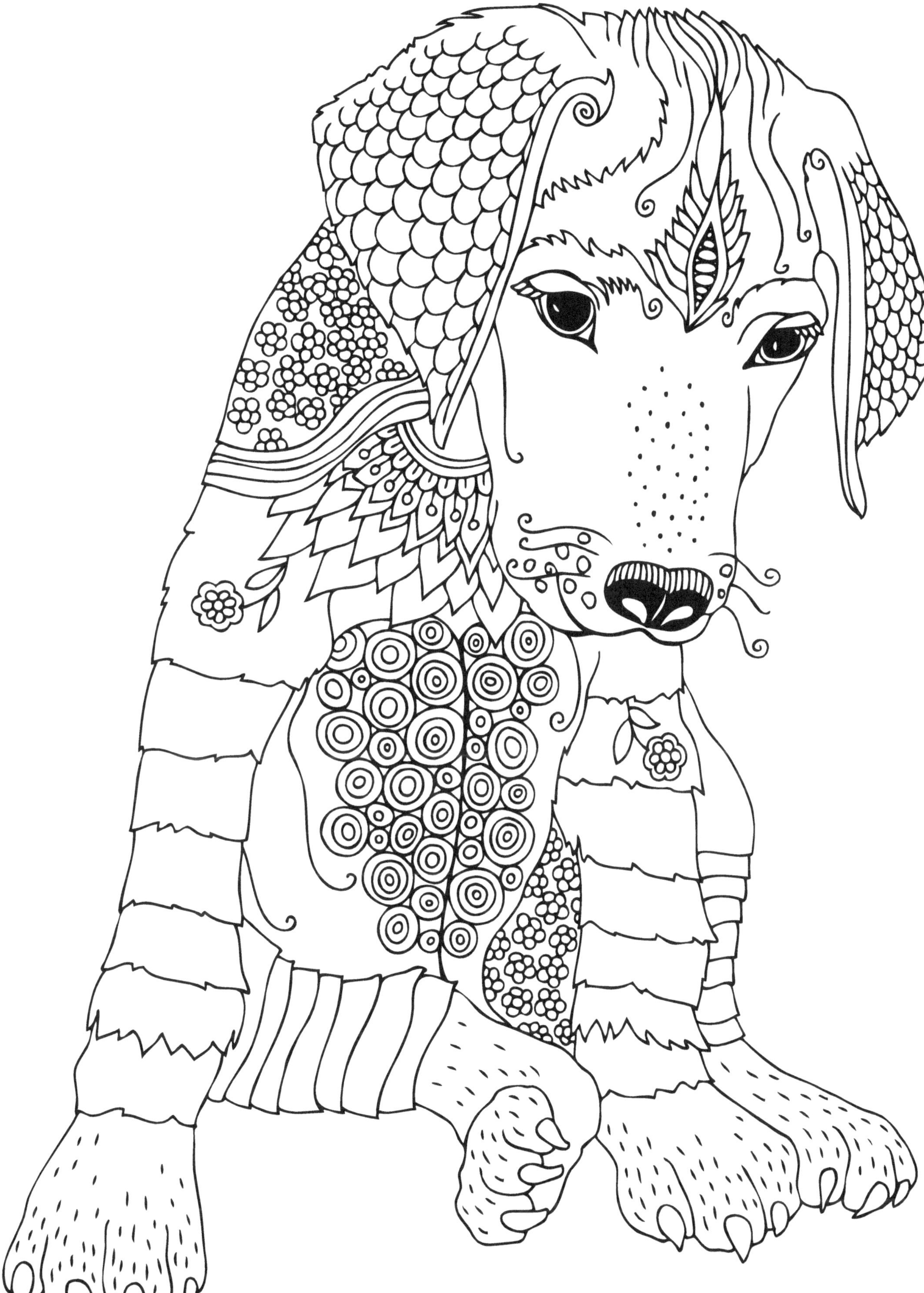

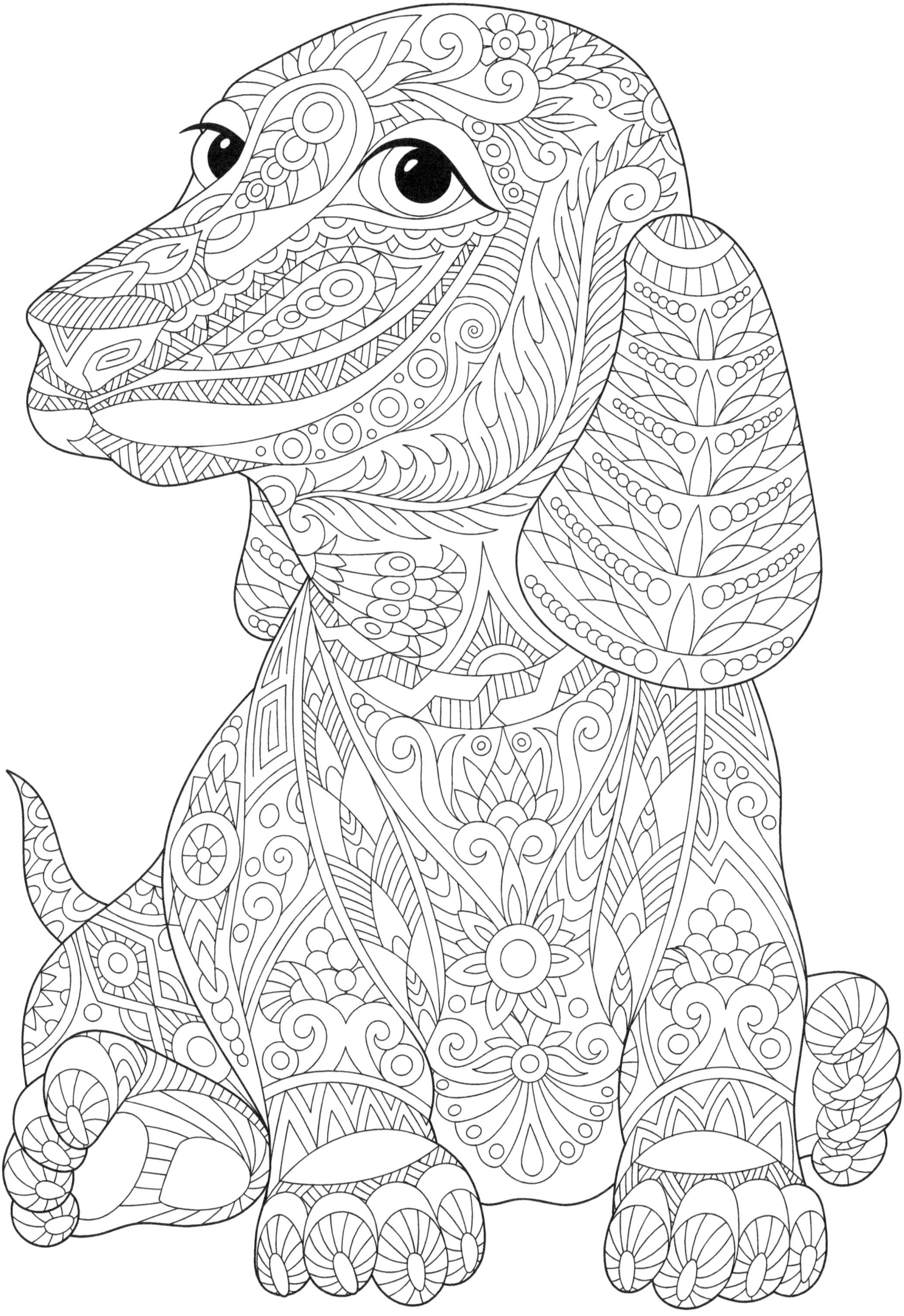

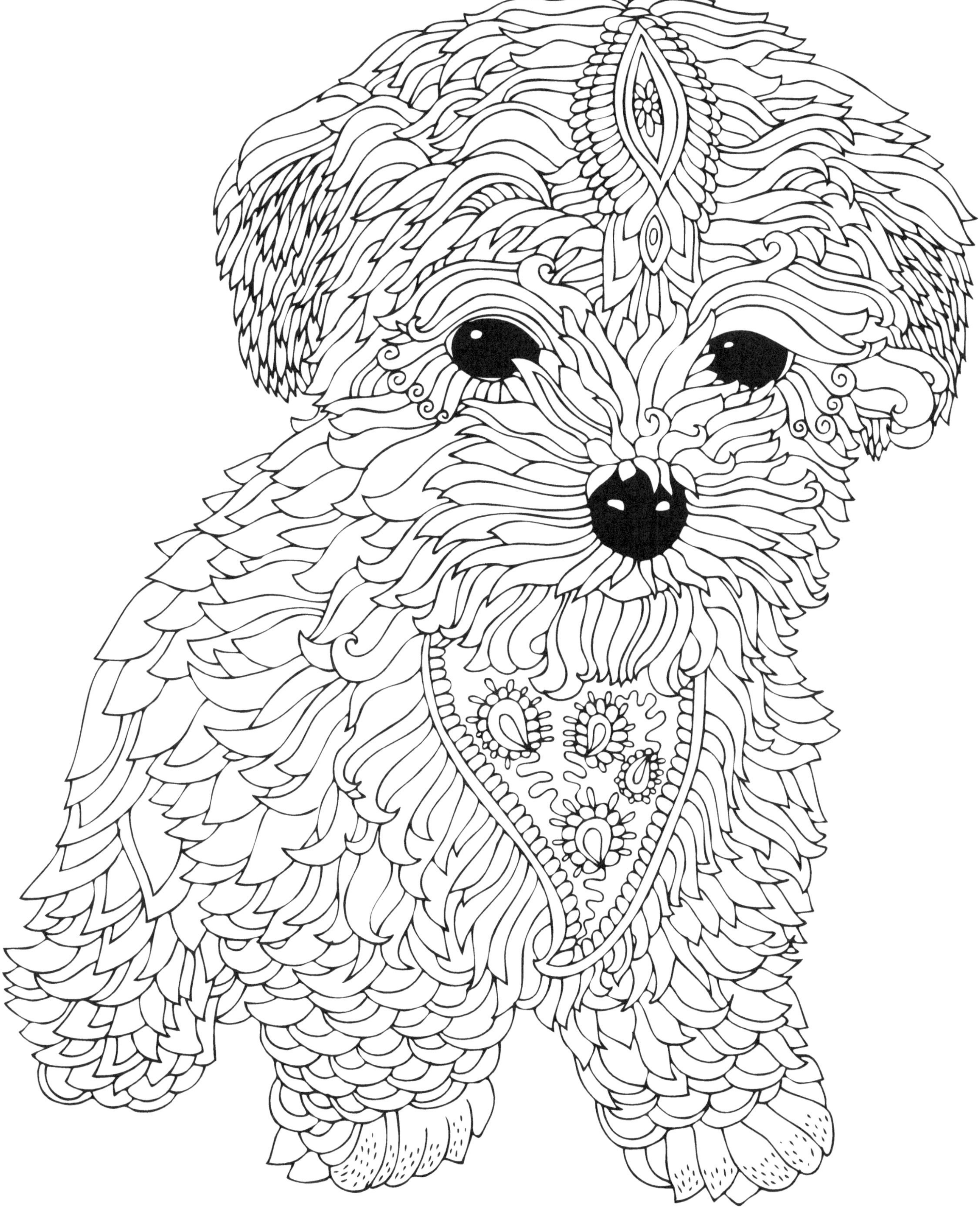

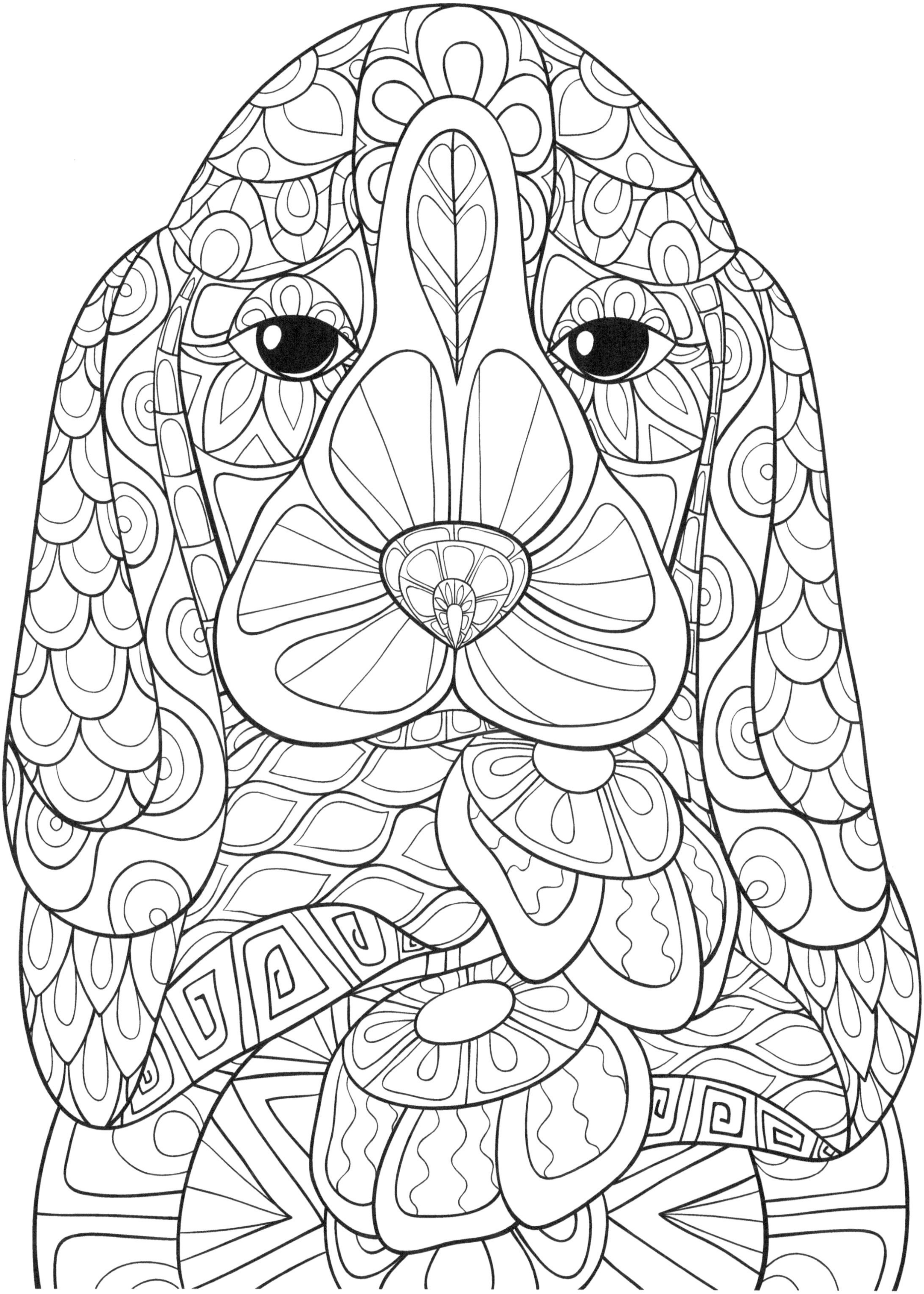

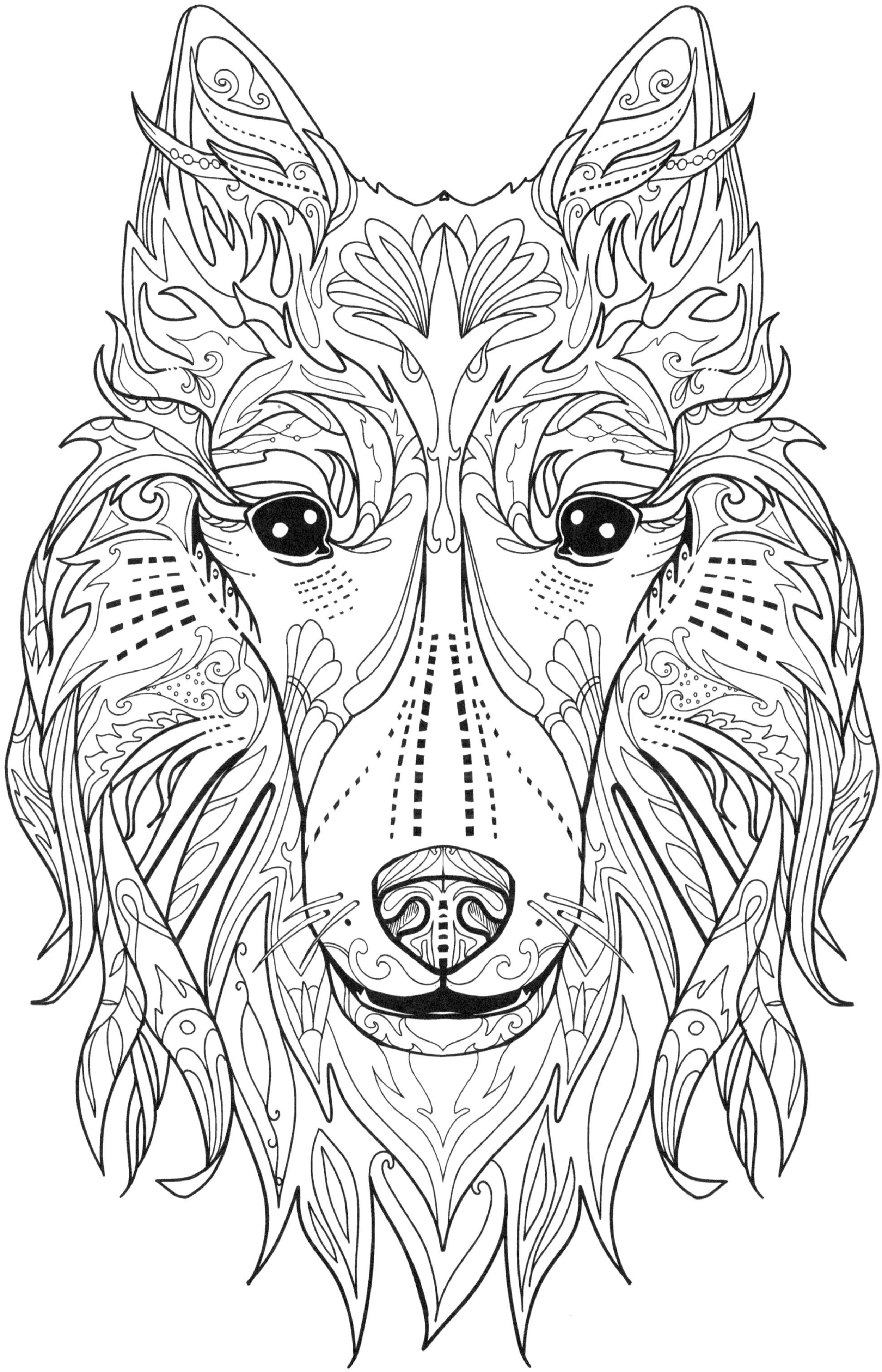

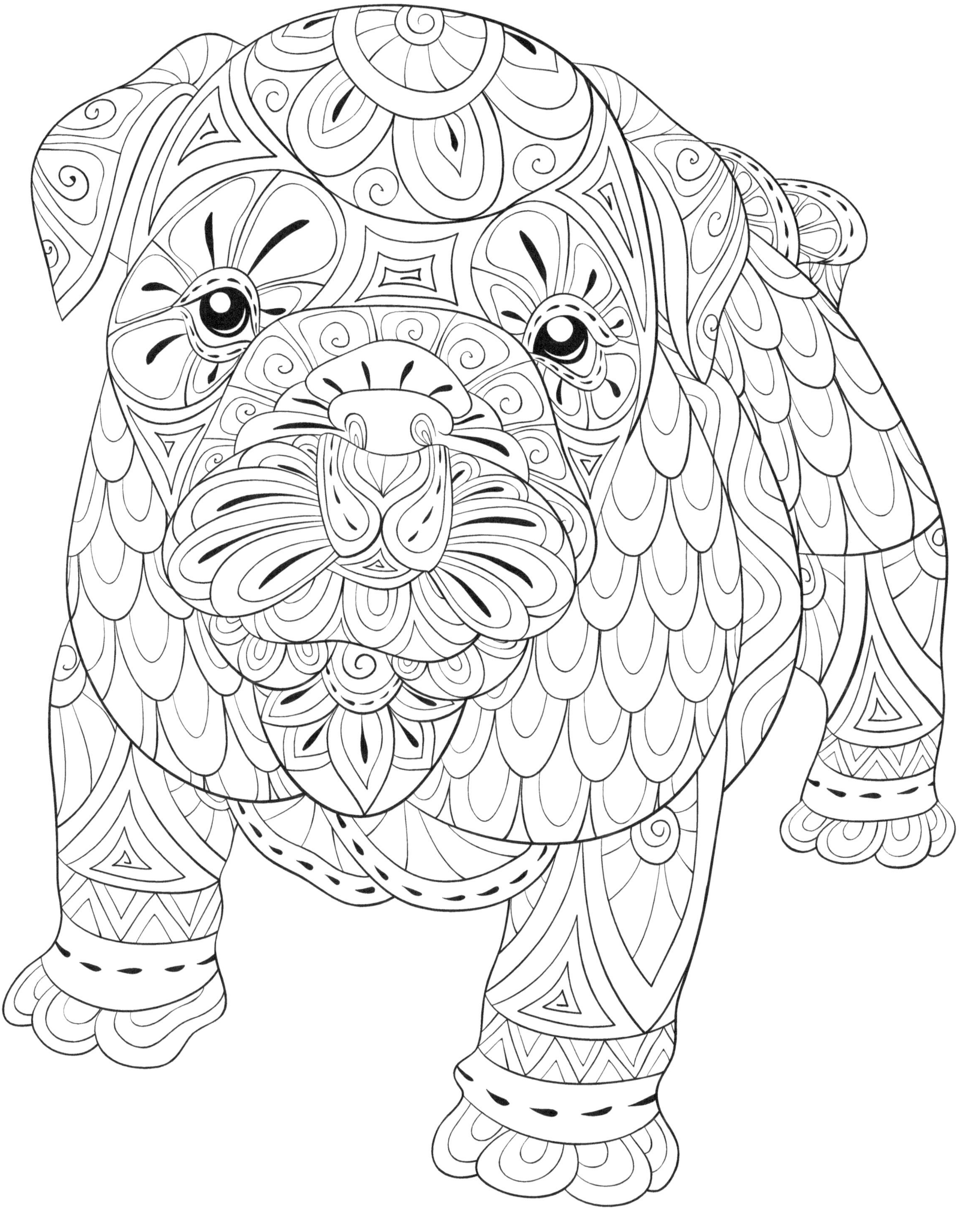

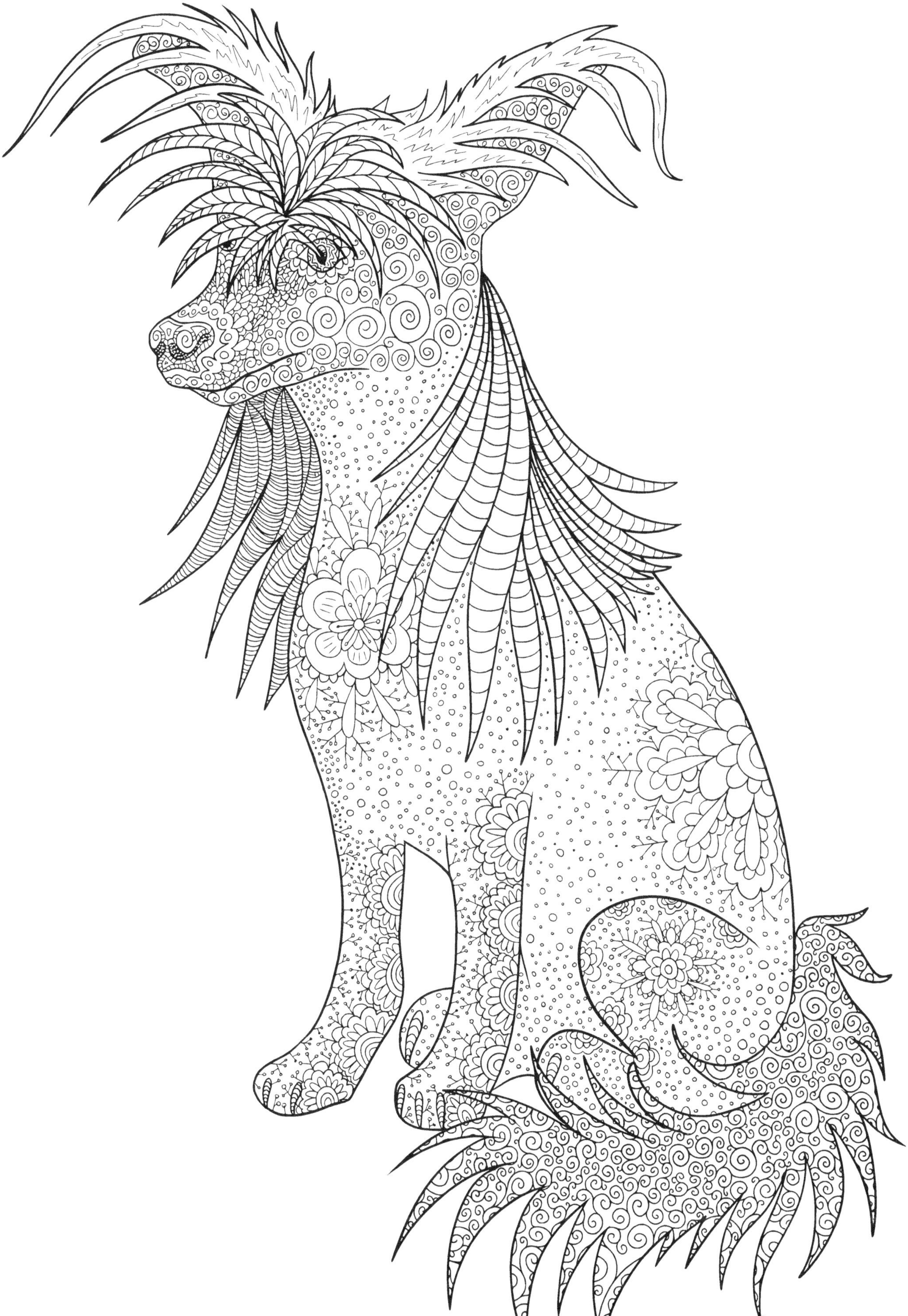

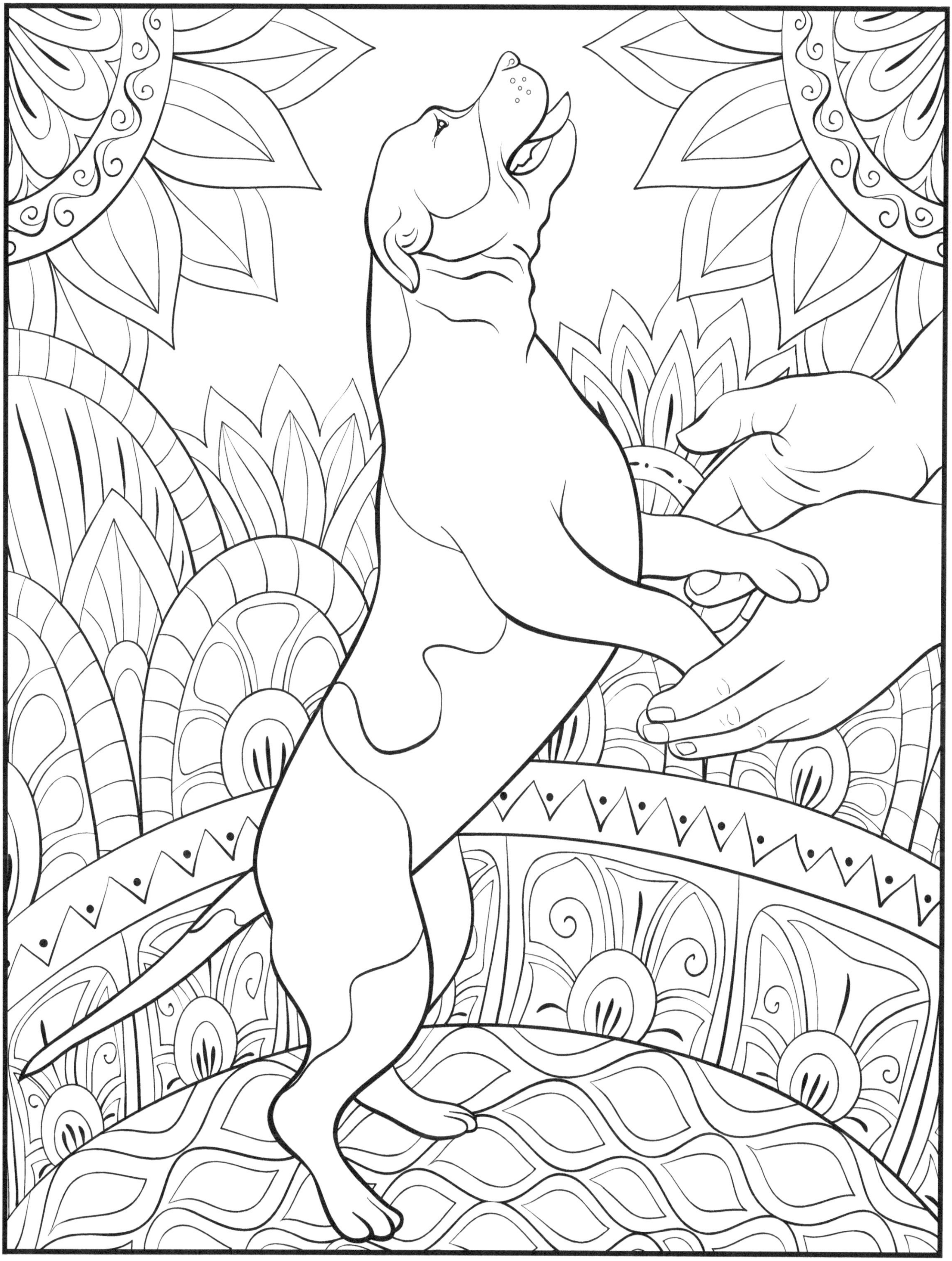

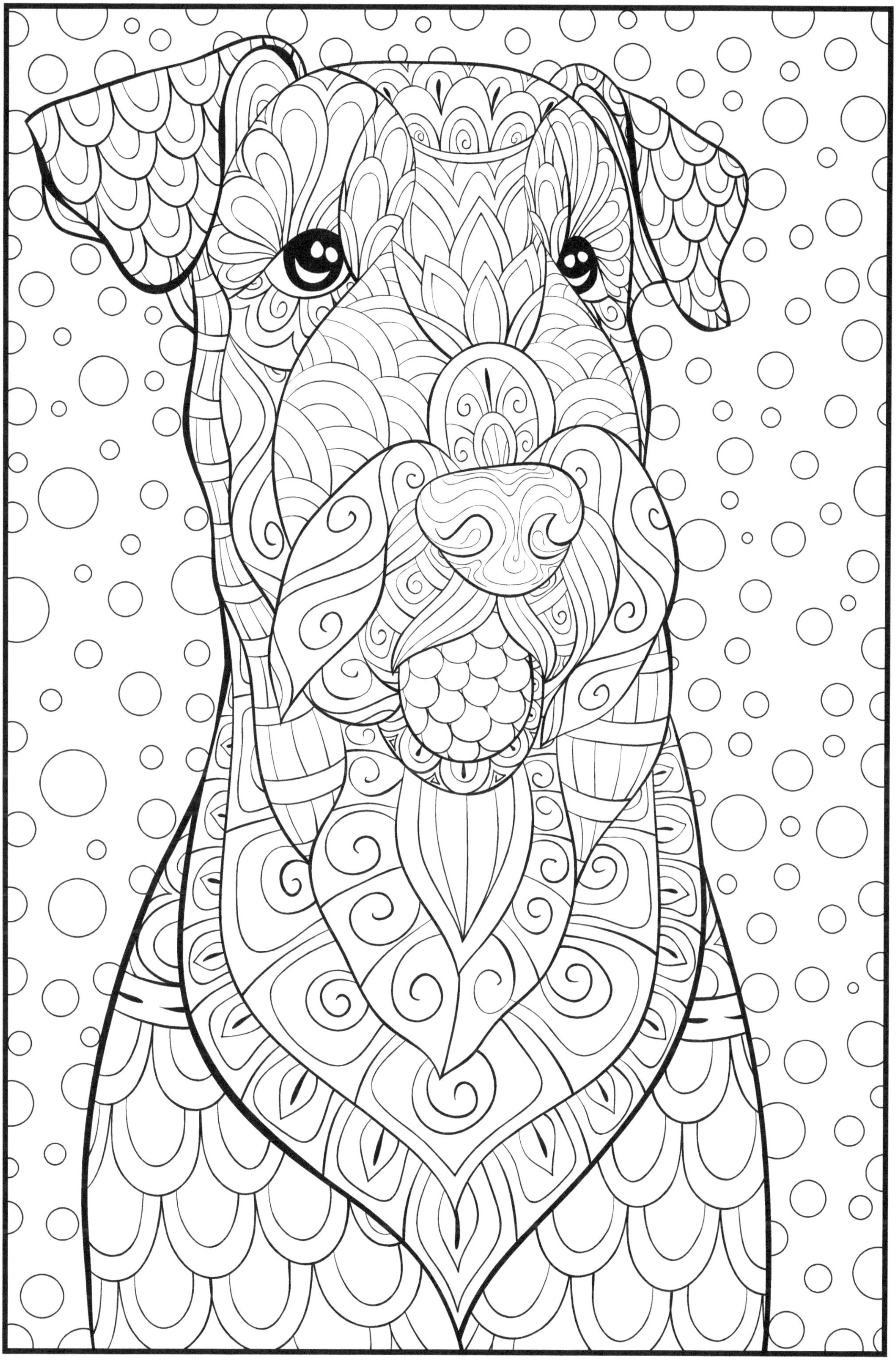

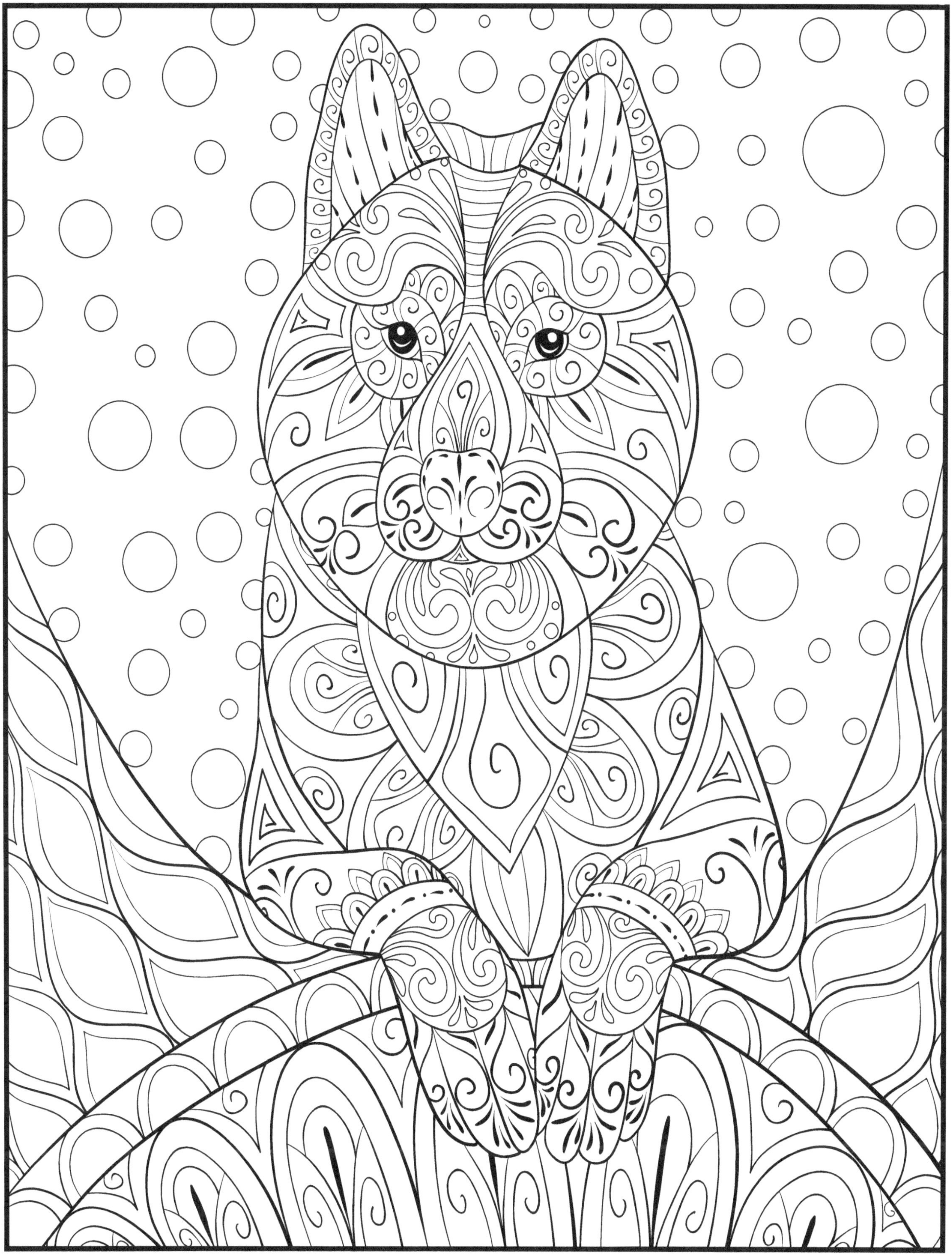

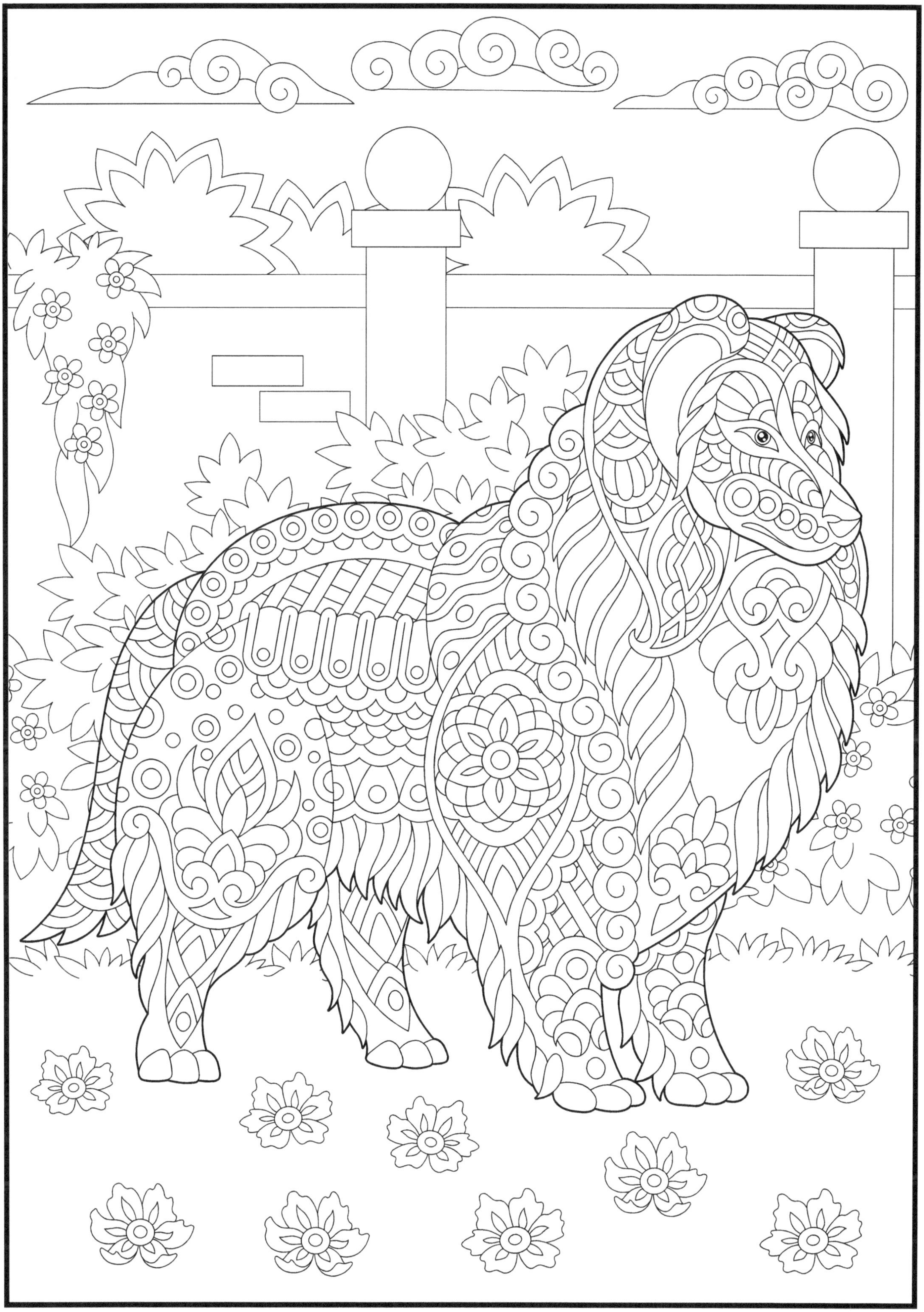

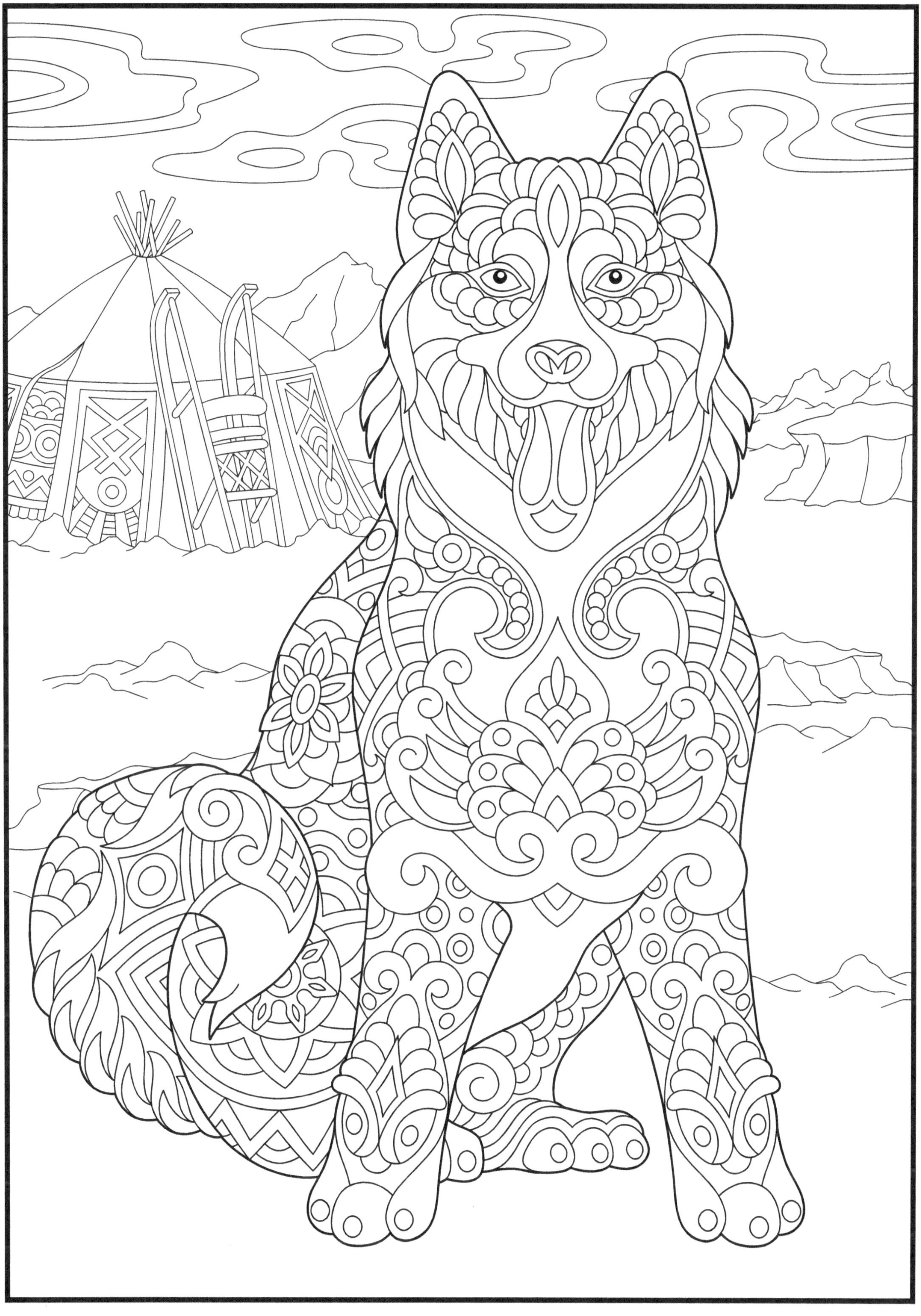

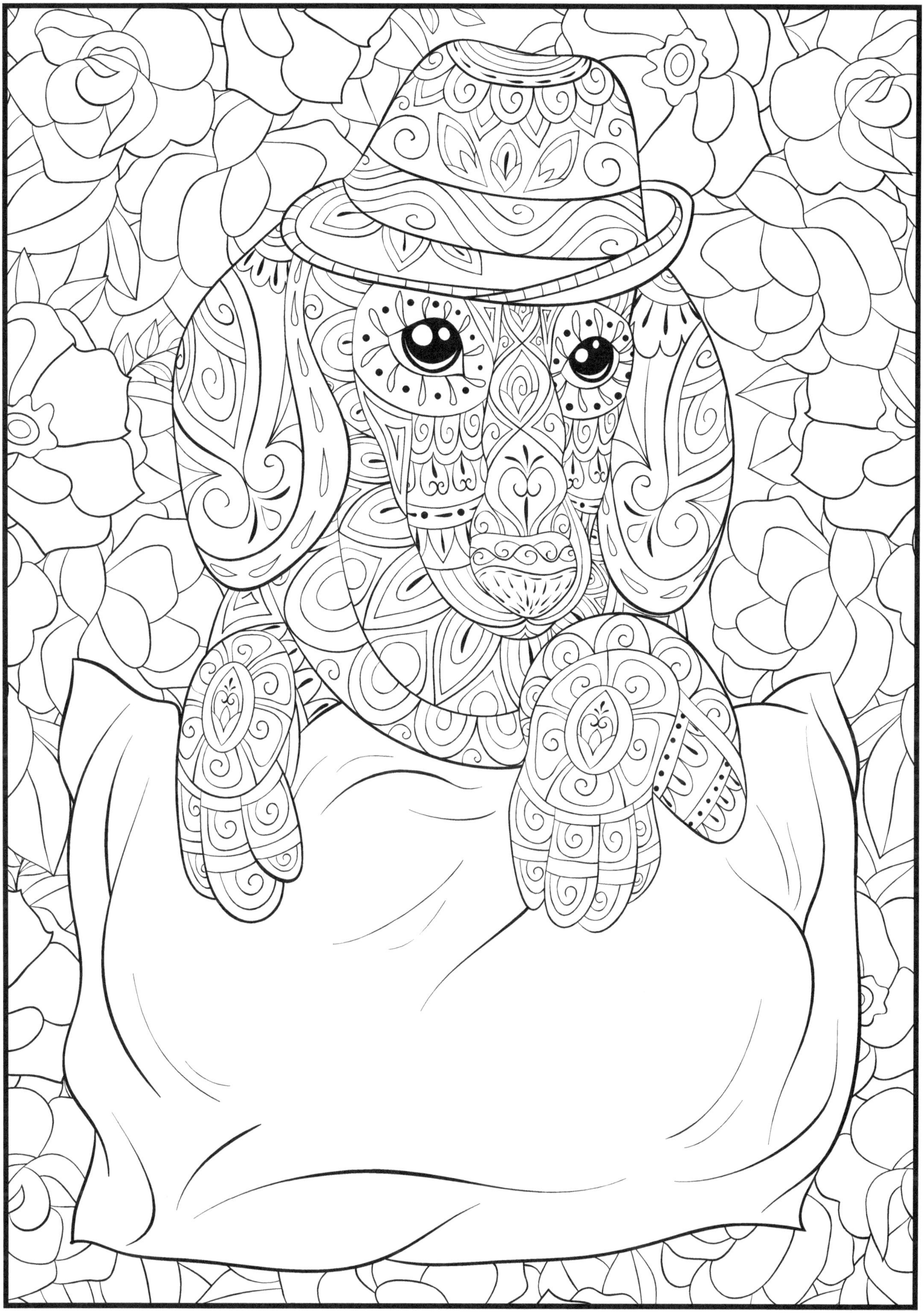

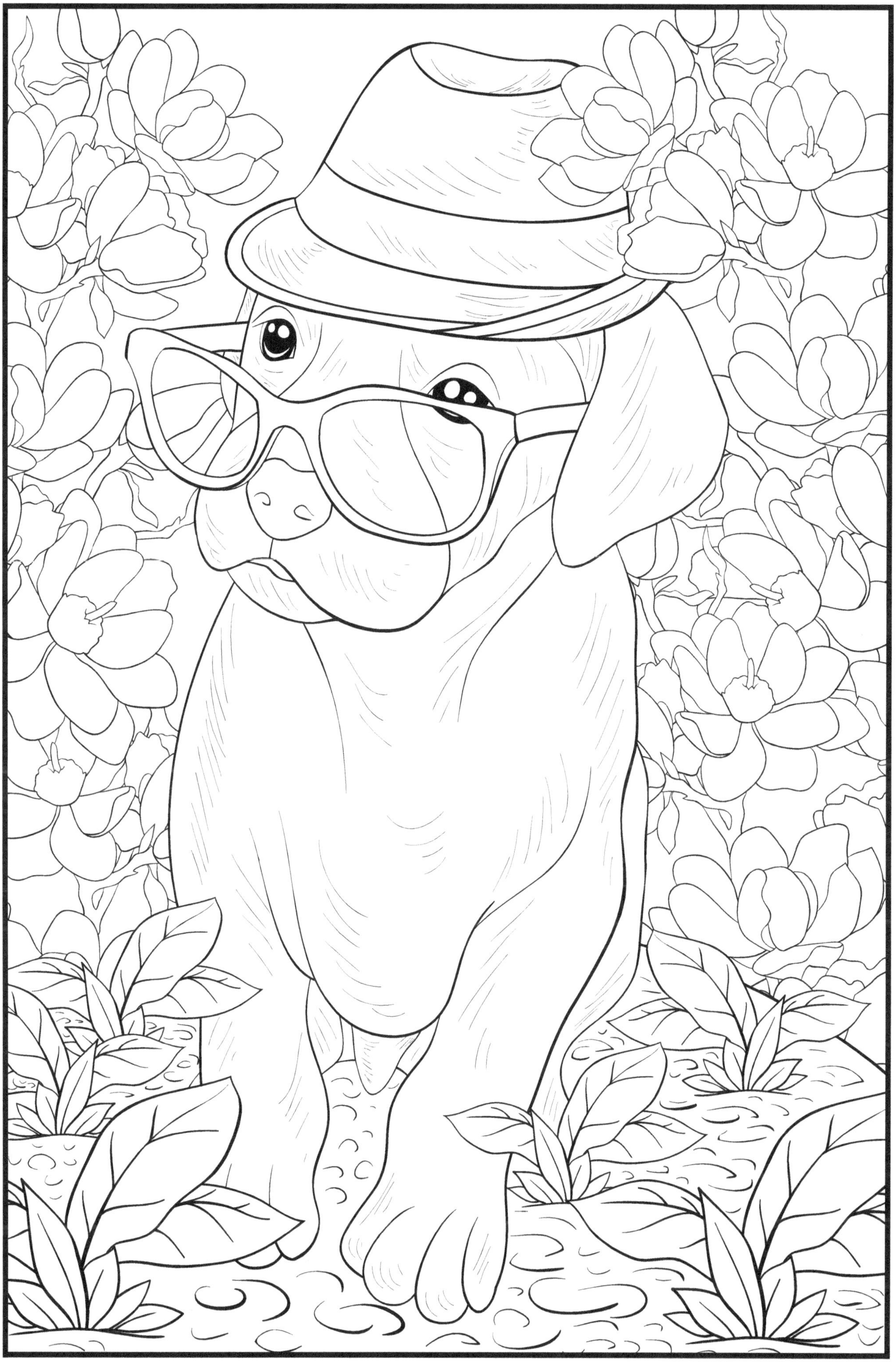

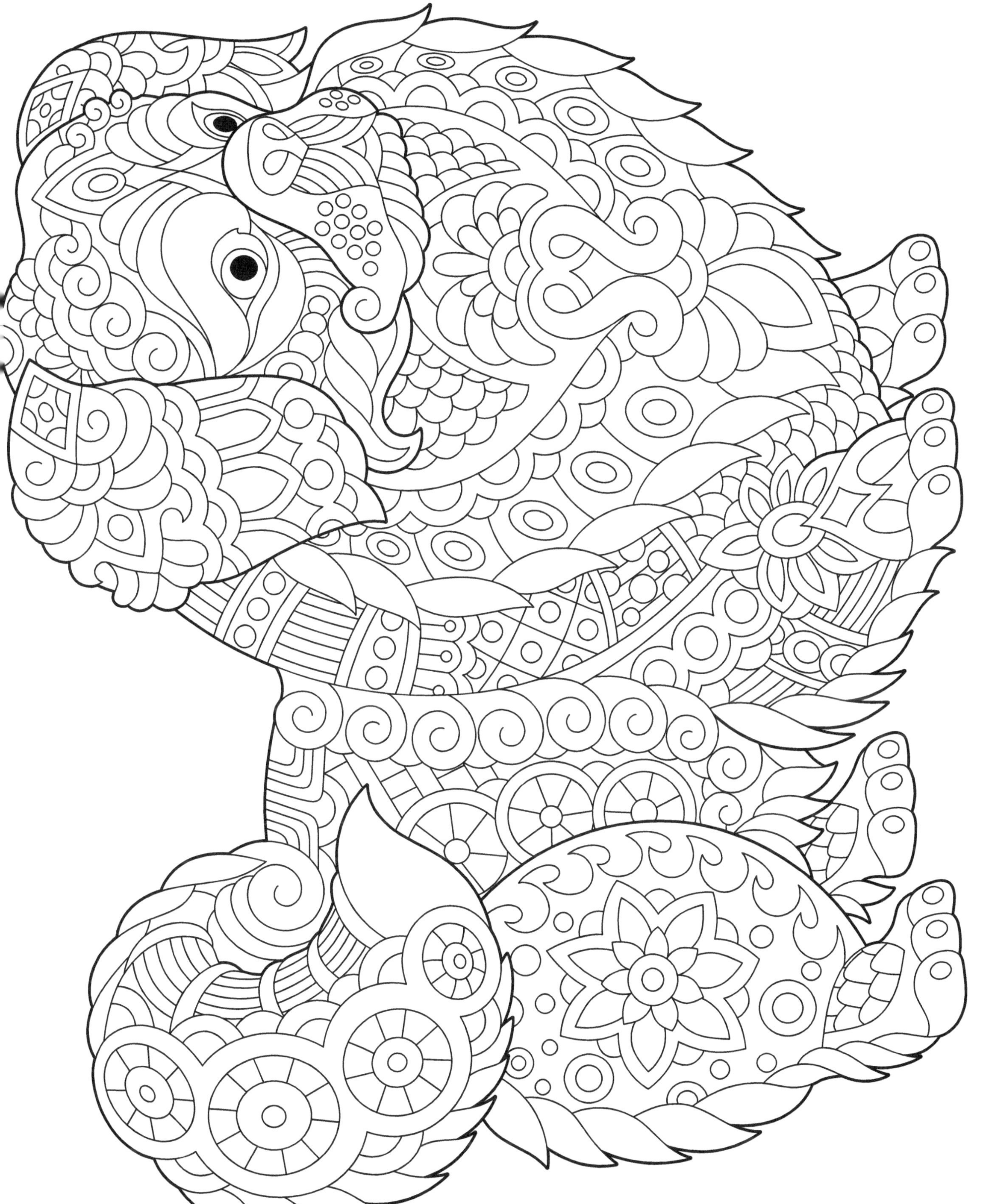

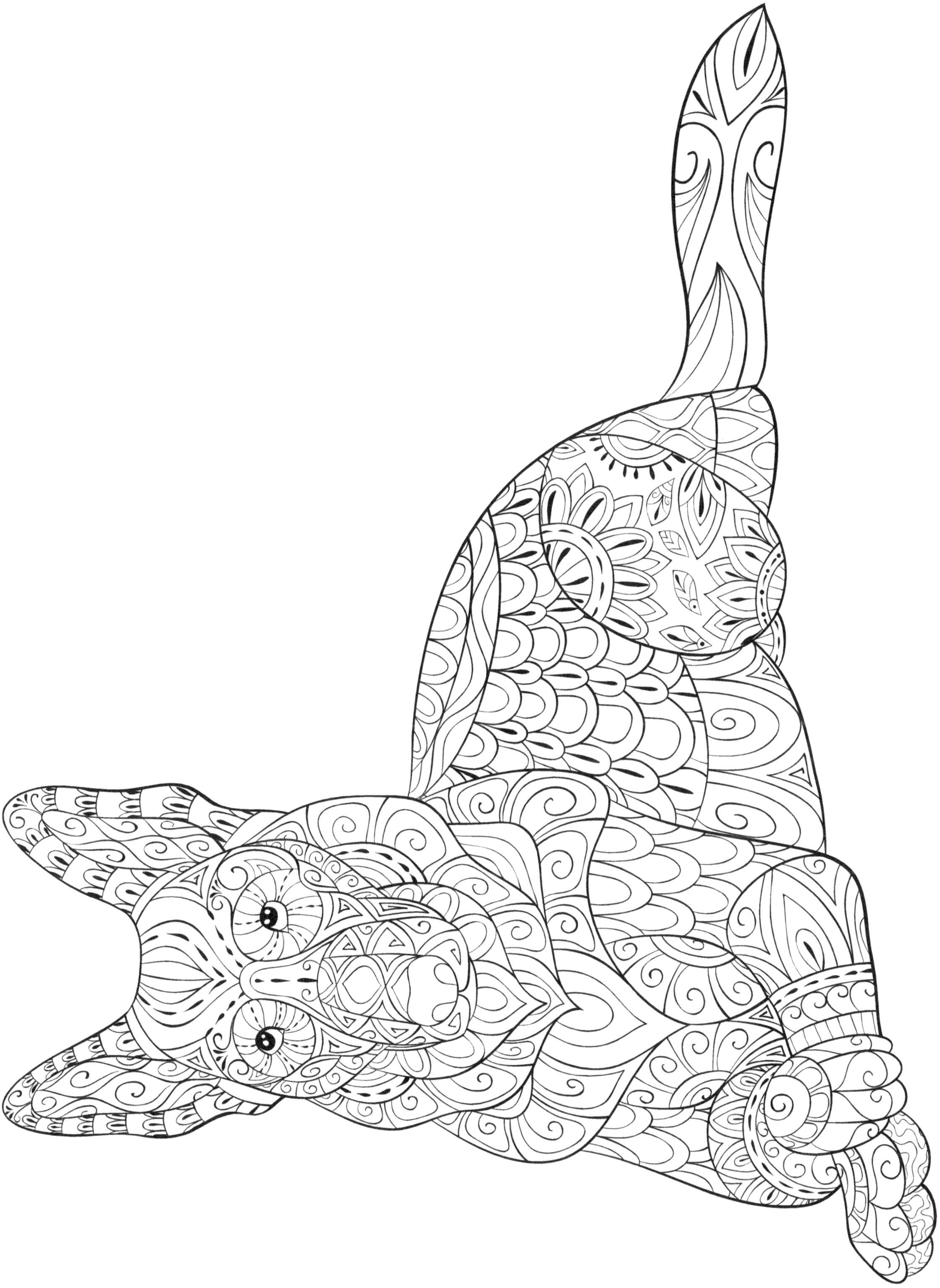

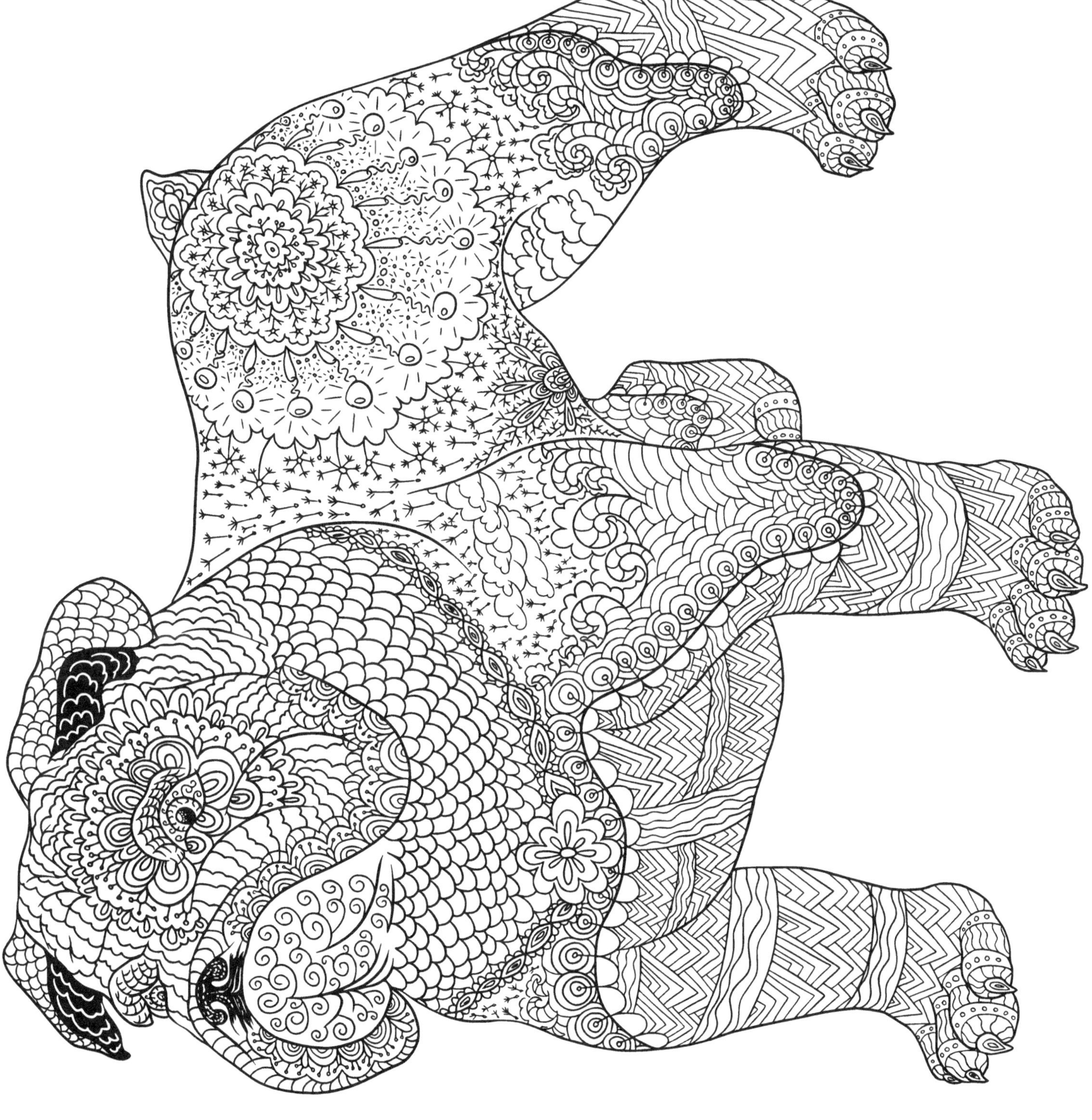

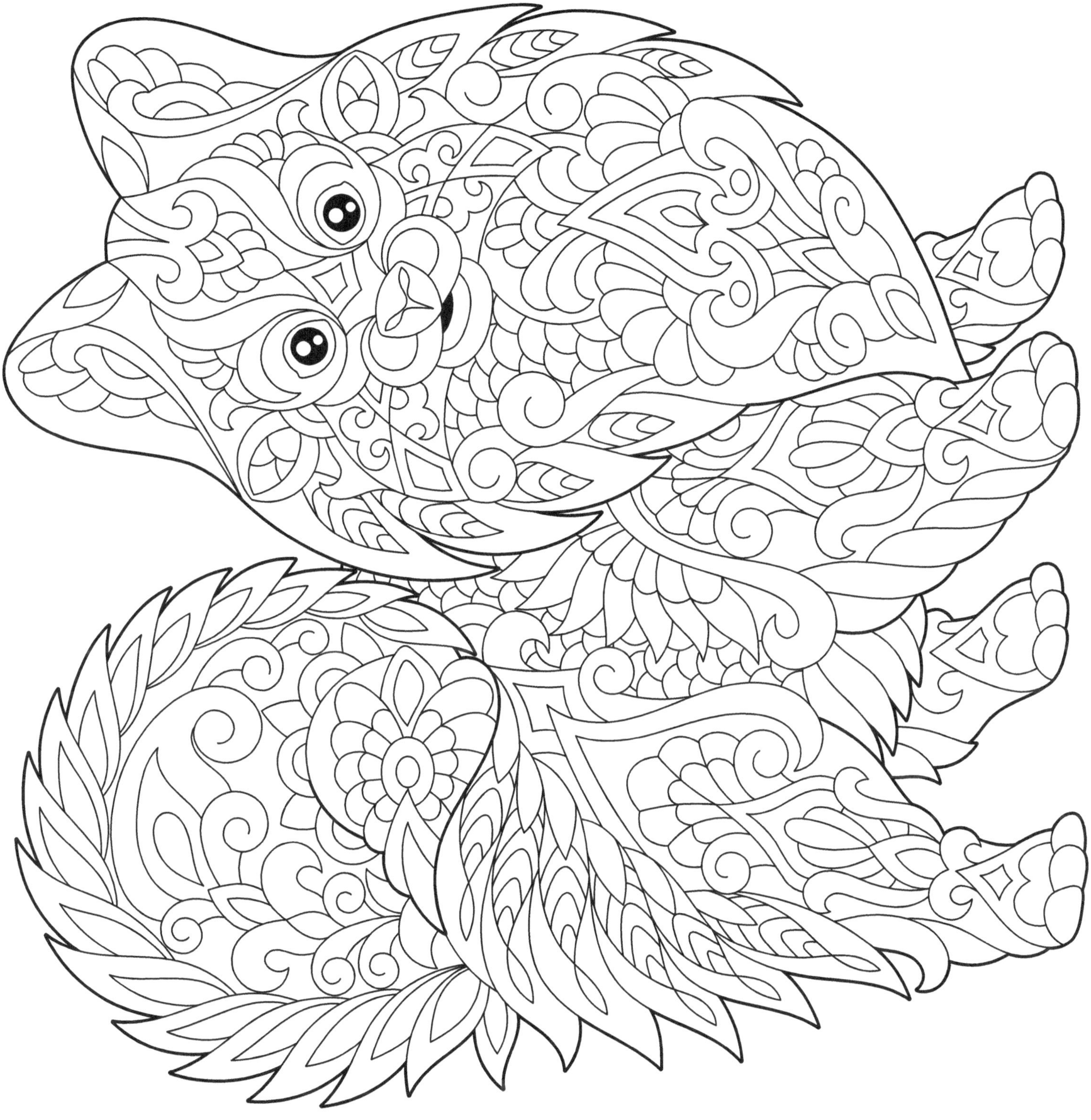

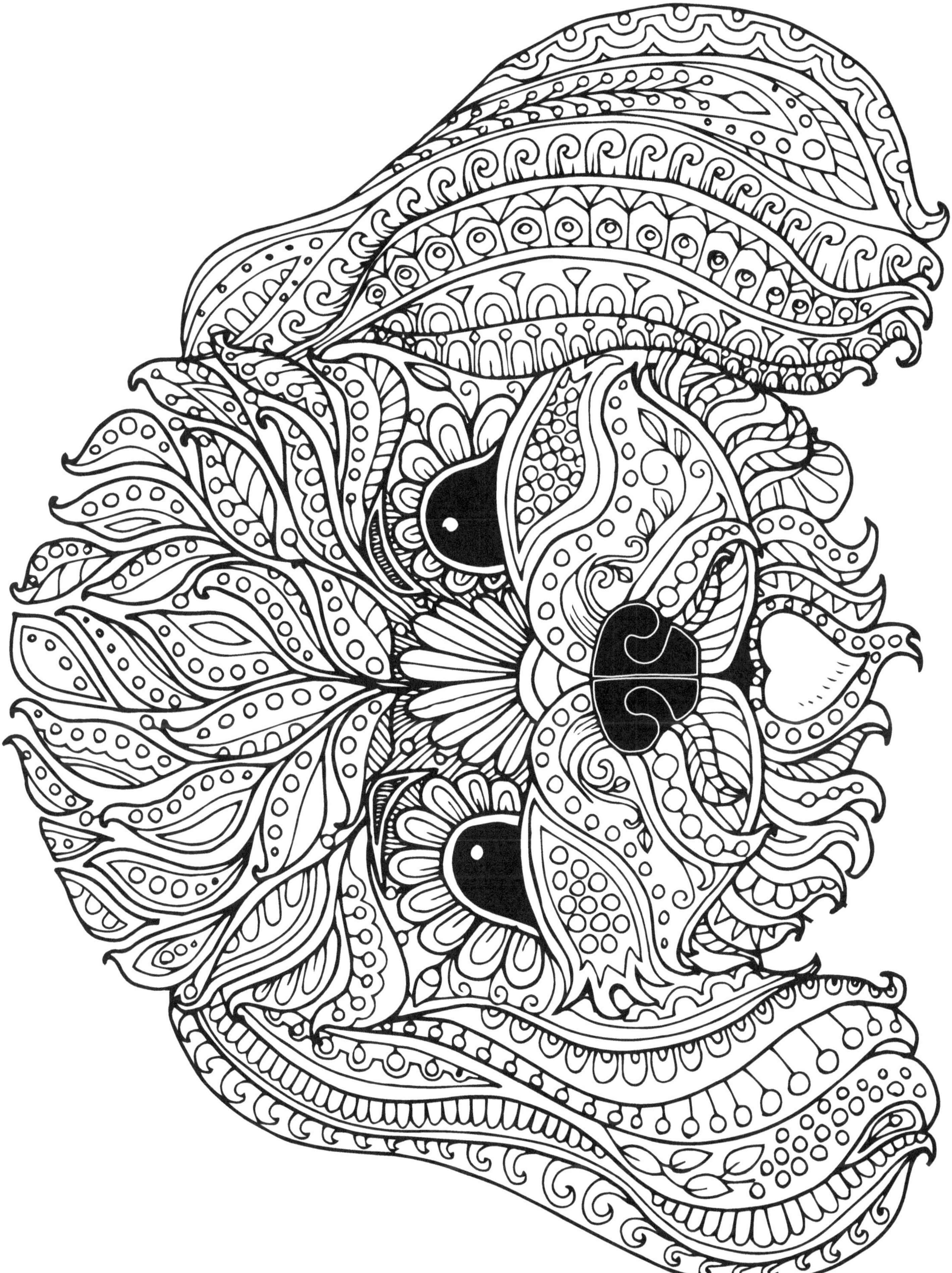

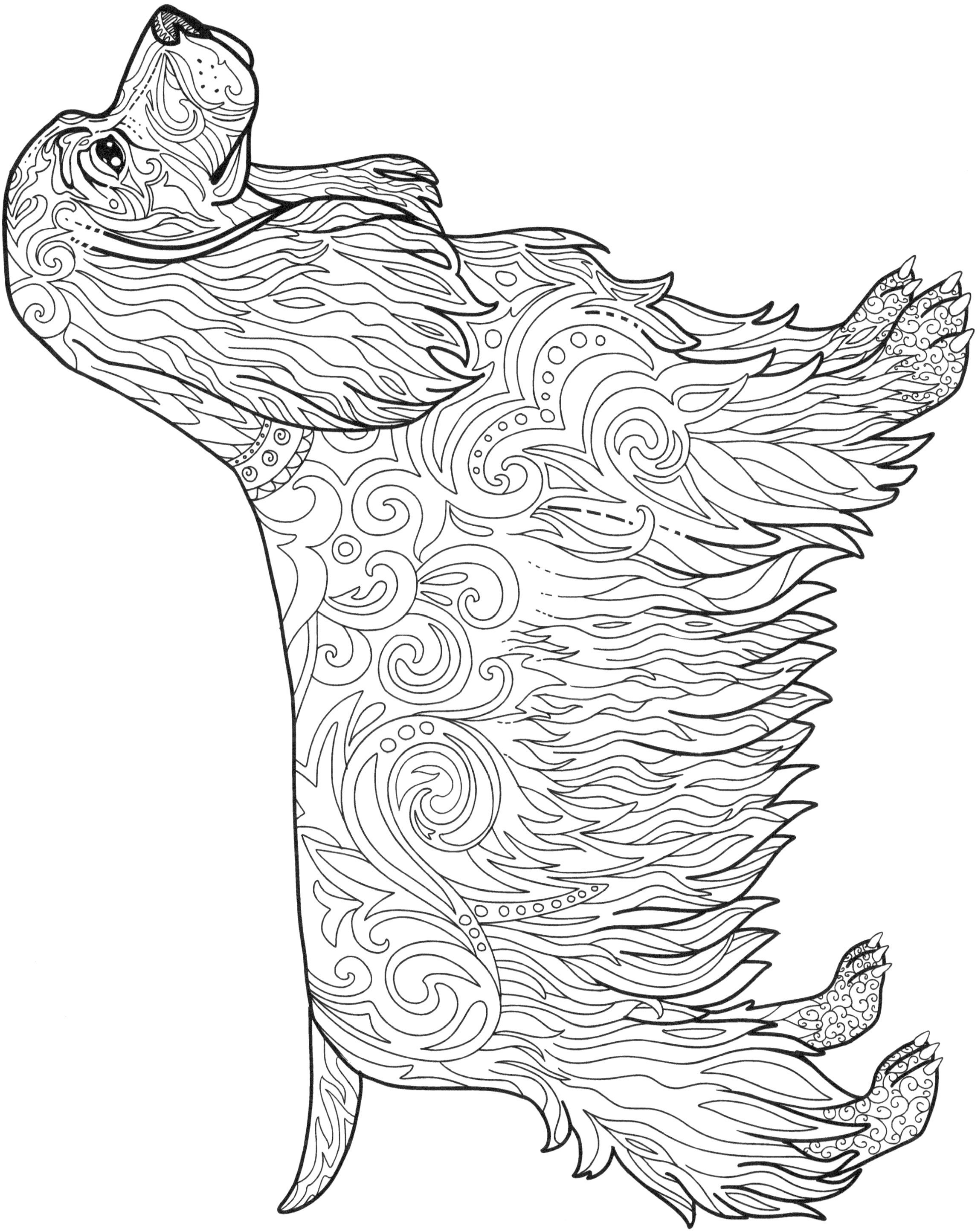

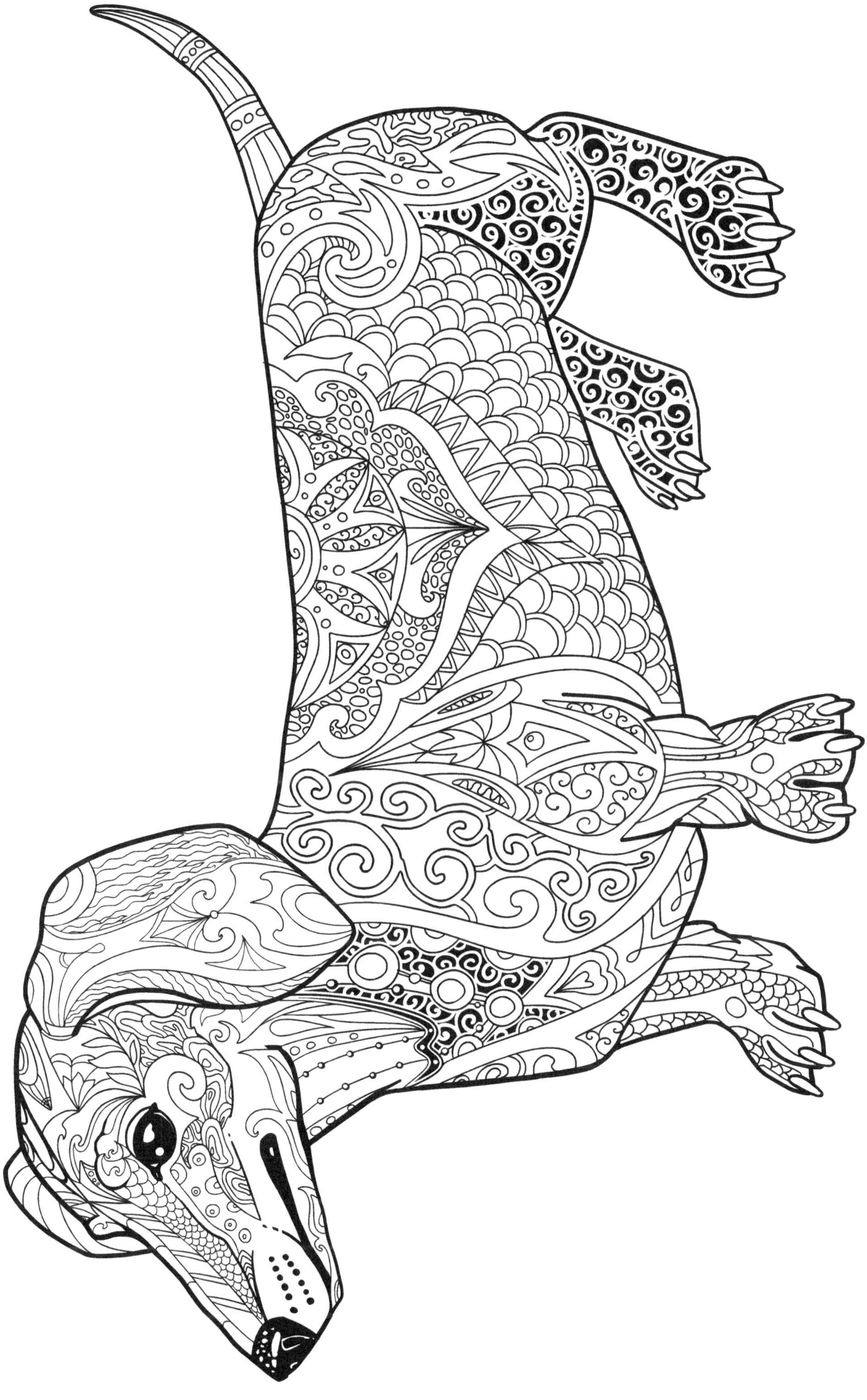

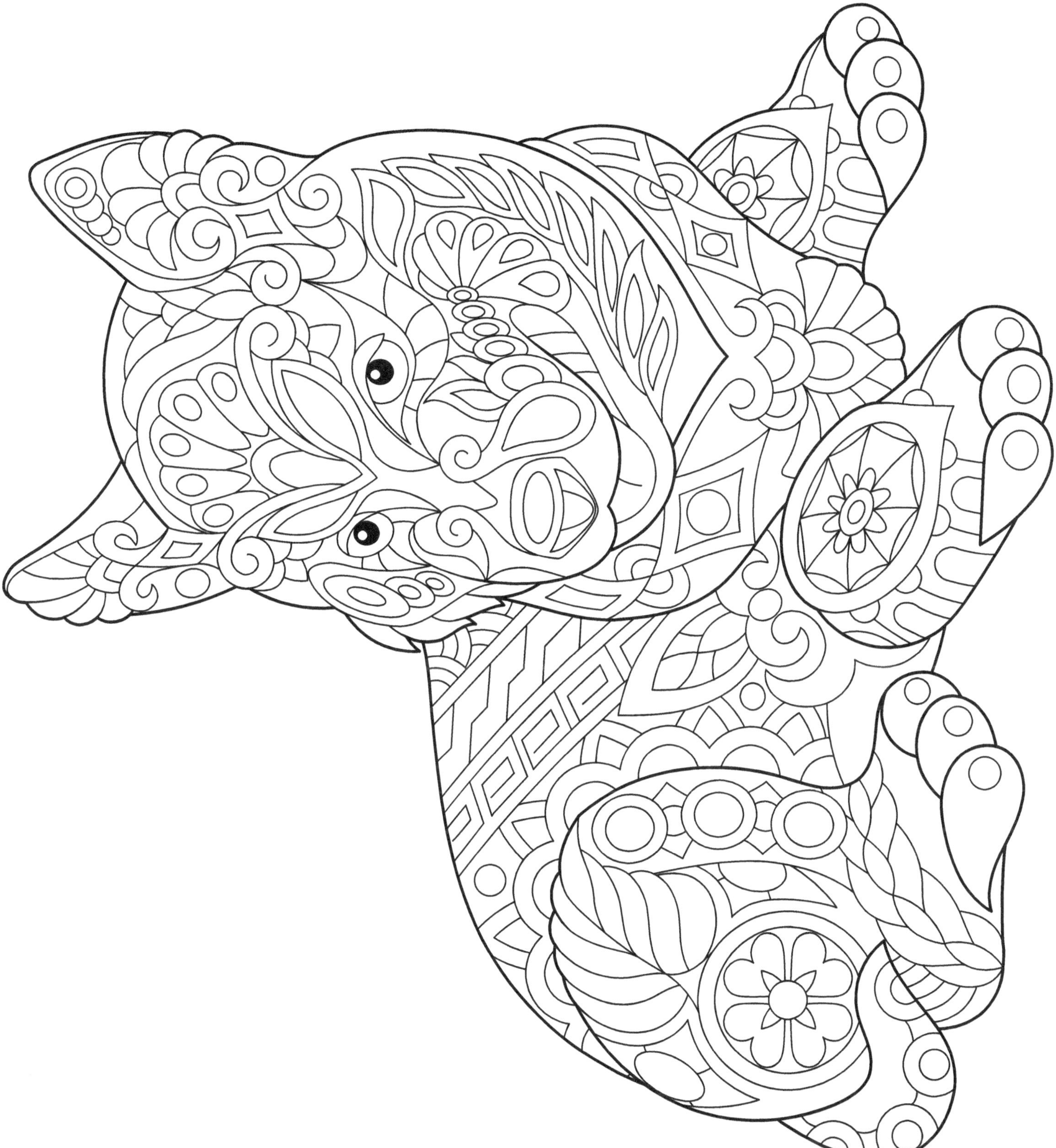

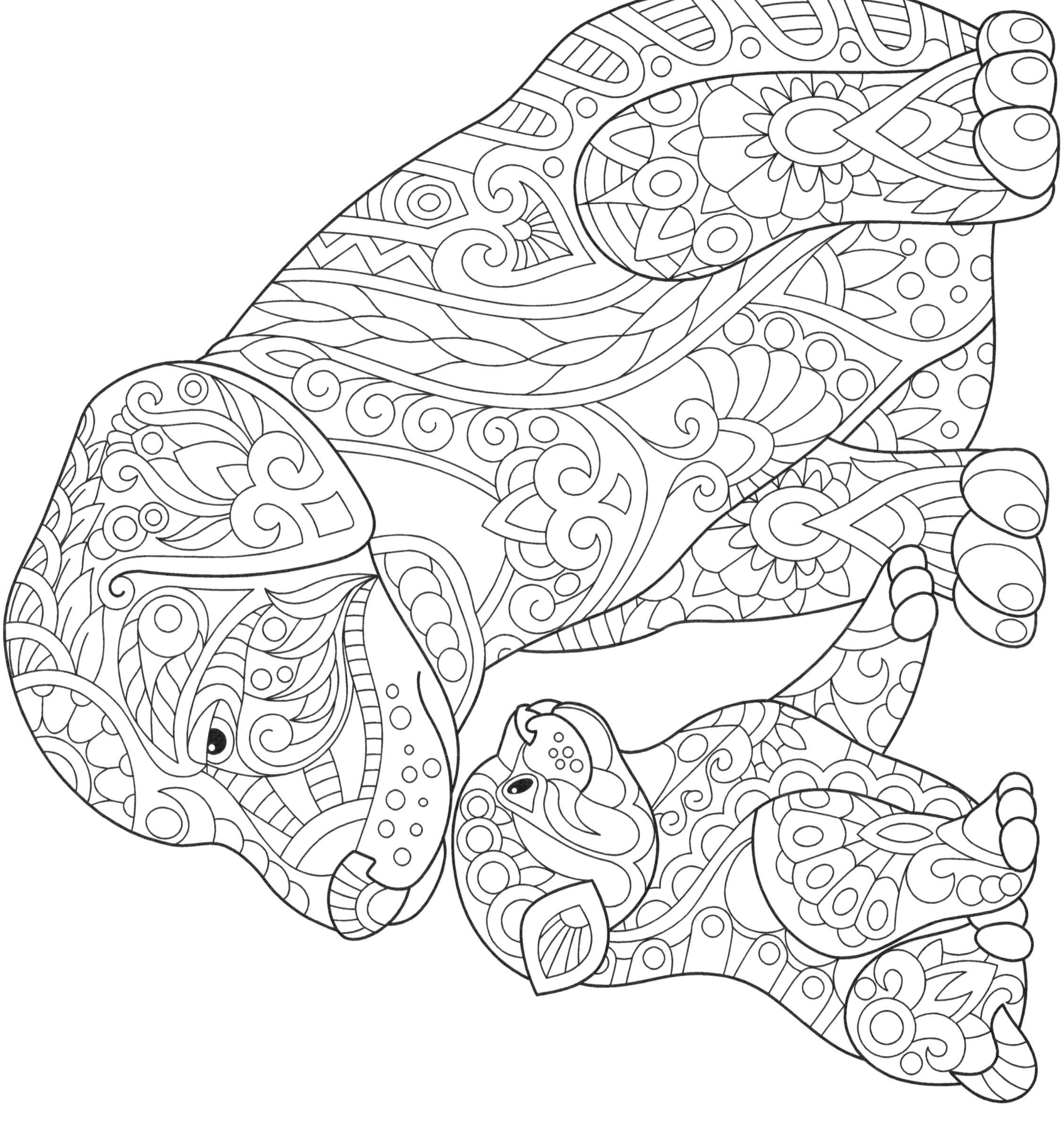

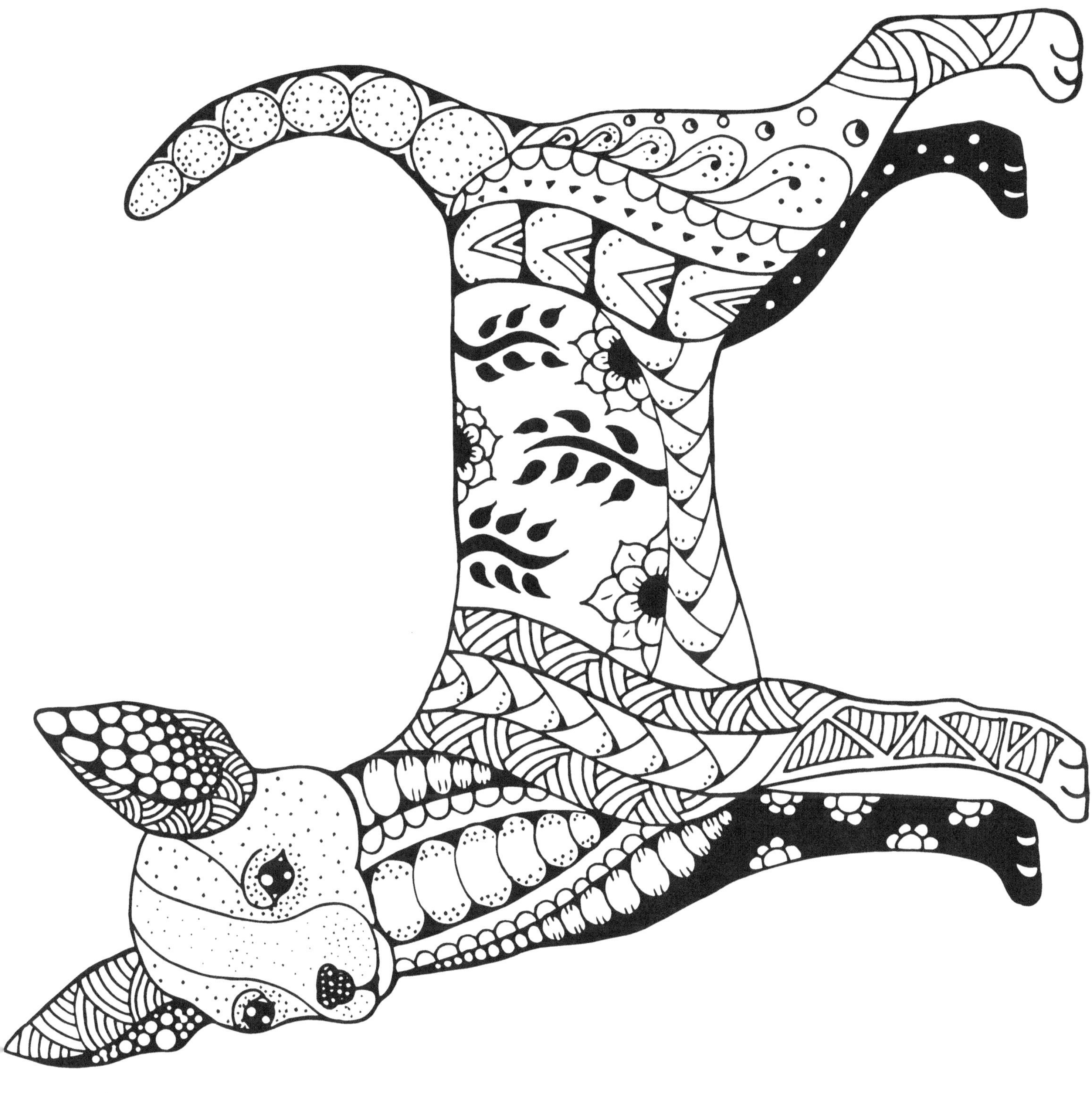

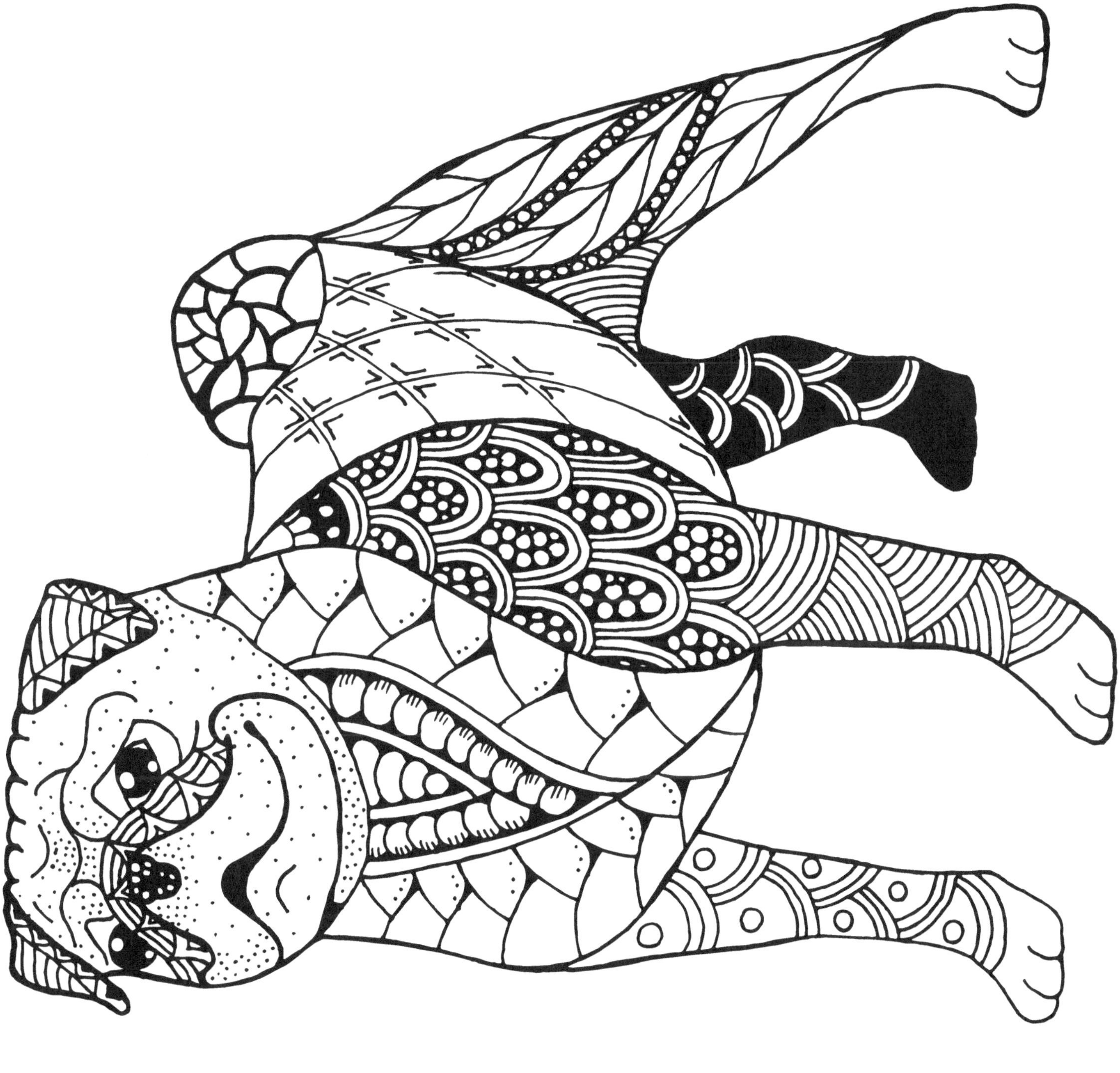

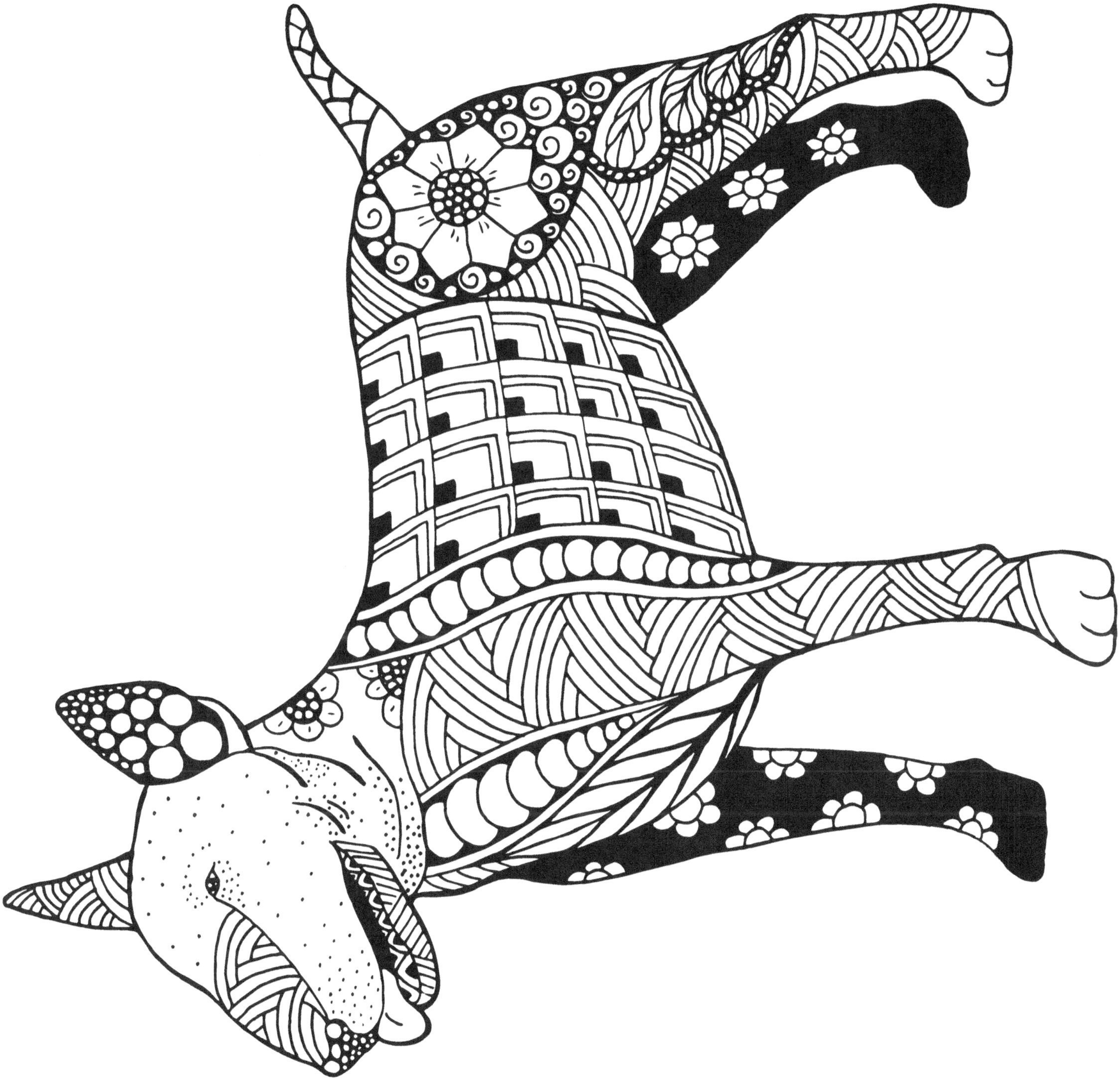

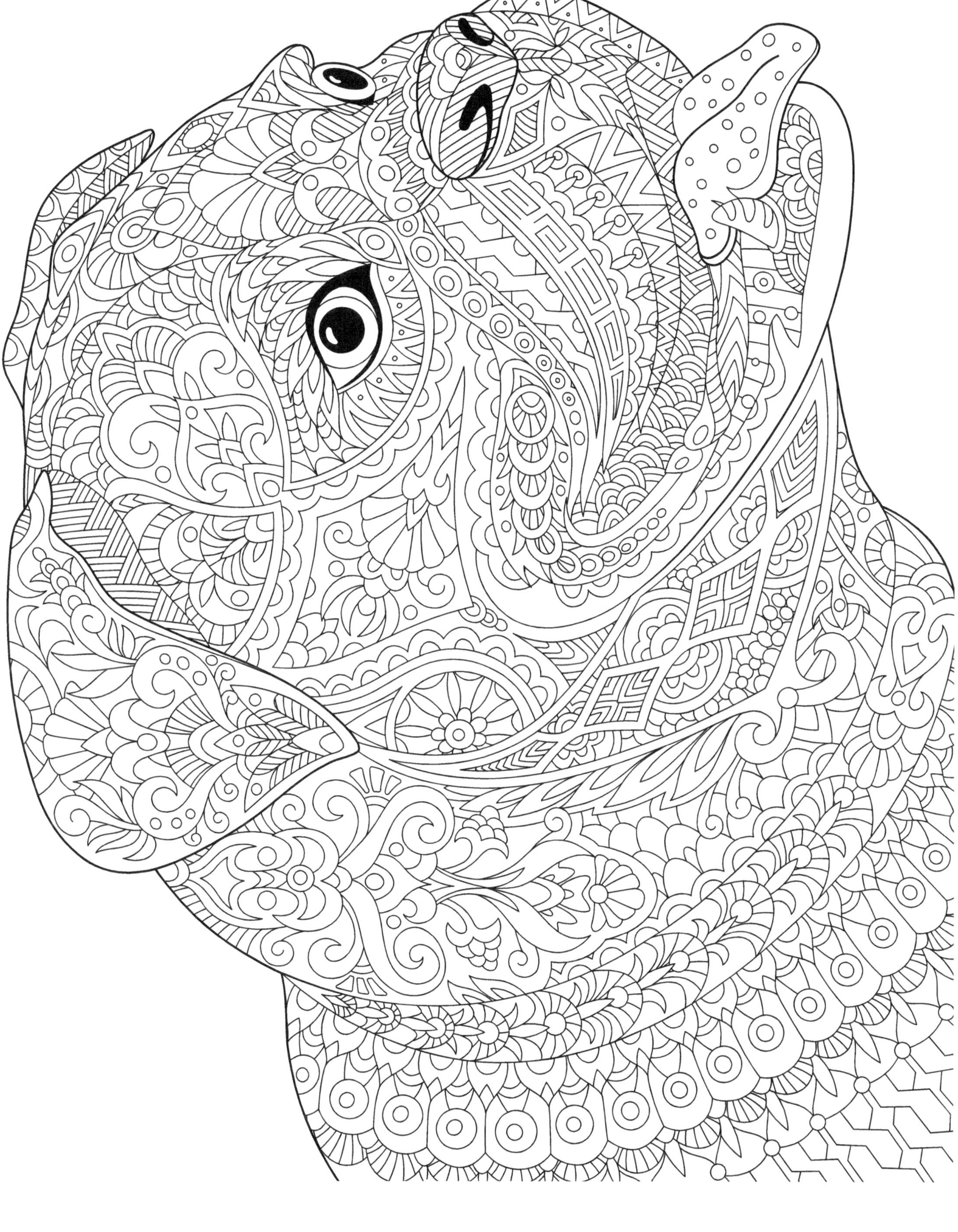

www.ingramcontent.com/pod-product-compliance
Lightning Source LLC
Chambersburg PA
CBHW081743220526
45468CB00008B/2222
9781721209866